SCHOOLING
AND
INNOVATION

THE RHETORIC
AND THE REALITY

ANGELA E. FRALEY

Tyler Gibson Publishers • *New York* • 1981

Library of Congress Cataloging Data

Fraley, Angela E.
  Schooling and Innovation: The Rhetoric and the Reality

  Includes index. Bibliography: p. 226-233

  1. Educational innovations — United States
LA217 .F7   1981   370.19 0973 19   81-169045

CONTENTS

FOREWORD

Dr. Fraley has written a much needed book. In a time that has become more ahistorical than ever in education, she reminds us that we continue to cycle back over the same questions, and come to the same conclusions, again and again.

The book was carefully researched over a ten year period. Some of the received wisdom from the period after 1870 is challenged by Dr. Fraley's findings—especially the relationship between Dewey and Parker, and the fate of the Gary Plan and the core curriculum. The major innovative efforts of the past hundred years are freshly described. Dr. Fraley's message is that, in the attempts to improve the schools, we should deal with continuities, not mere inspiration.

Teachers College   ARTHUR W. FOSHAY
Columbia University   *Professor Emeritus*

PREFACE

This is a book about school as a social institution in the United States. The school reformers in the nineteenth and twentieth centuries promoted the ideal of schools to teach democratic citizenship. Drawing their vision from the founding fathers, highly talented and dedicated people exhausted every conceivable refinement of rhetoric or practice that might have contributed to establishing the democratic school. In spite of this thoroughness, the ideal has never been achieved, because the limitations of school as a social institution confine the offering and the outcome to what can be accomplished in a classroom or similar school facility.

The records of four enterprises—Francis Parker and the derivative Dewey school, the Gary schools, core curriculum, and the Ford Foundation projects—document the thoroughness with which reformers have searched for a workable process to change schools into miniature democratic societies. These records reveal almost identical aims, programs, methods, claims of success, unsolvable problems, public criticism, and admissions of failure. Each enterprise dealt similarly with aims to turn schools into youth communities, with the means projected to accomplish the aims, and with the outcomes as reality in the existing institution of school. These four enterprises have been chosen as examples, not because their undertakings were unique, but because they attracted sufficient money and notoriety to become almost fully documented.

Francis W. Parker's work in Quincy, Massachusetts, in 1875 was the first widely publicized effort to accomplish democratic schooling in the United States, and he carried his ideas to the practice school of the Cook County Normal School in Chicago in 1883. The famous laboratory school opened by John Dewey in 1896 was patterned after the practice school. It dealt with the same stated aims in the same ways, but had a staff ratio of one teacher for every four children, thus approximating tutorial instruction with very small groups.

Following on these in 1908, attempting to apply Dewey's prescriptions in a city system of public schools, William Wirt gained national recognition with his work in Gary, Indiana. He proved the economic feasibility of providing a range of educational experiences exceeding Dewey's, providing them much more professionally, and to large classes, but giving up some of the small group attention in exchange for an unprecedented freedom of pupil choice.

With the 1920s came the effort to define school practices that would insure an outcome of democratic-thinking-and-acting citizens. In support of this idea, starting in 1932, the Progressive Education Association spent ten years and approximately $800,000 on the Eight-Year Study, freeing selected schools to experiment with *progressive* schooling. They hoped to find a set of recommendations that any teacher could act upon and thereby produce in the classroom a cooperative group enterprise that would serve the multiple ends of basic skills mastery, pursuit of intellectual interests, participatory democratic social experience, and self-confidence to face and resolve life problems. This was promoted as core curriculum. Follow-up research was disappointing. Ten years later the only identifiable change traceable to the effort was the professional growth of the people who served as project supervisors and who went on to higher administrative or college teaching jobs.

In the early 1950s, the post-World War II pressure for schooling to preserve democracy brought numerous experimental programs to improve schools while coping with a serious shortage of certified teachers. Educators were sure they knew what to do if only they had the money to do it. The Ford Foundation called them to task. Through the Fund for the Advancement of Education and the Comprehensive School Improvement Program, Ford grants for the next twenty years, in effect, gave financial *carte blanche* to selected projects to prove their worth and viability. Grants amounted to fifty million dollars the first decade for "short term pilot plant efforts" to support the ideas "that seemed to offer at least partial solutions to problems plaguing American schools and colleges" with the hope of identifying desirable changes. Grants amounting to thirty million dollars the second decade funded attempts to concentrate enough new practices in the same school to demonstrate a marked difference in the schooling offered. The outcomes, assessed by the Foundation in 1970, echoed the experiences of the Eight-Year Study.

School is only one of many social institutions, all of which influence the attitudes and actions of people simultaneously. When school reformers insist that the school can educate in a way that will counteract or redirect the existing social order, they raise expectations that can not be realized. Further, they divert attention and energies from the primary task of the school, the task of producing an informed and inquiring citizenry.

Educators must accept the fact that more is lost than is gained in attempts to govern schools by democratic group process which ideally allows freedom of choice, including the choice not to participate. Since attendance is compulsory, if that choice is made, even by a few, the result is neither democracy nor school. It is confusion. Something prevents any radical changes in the governance of school. Perhaps it is the fact that school is school, not a total life experience for children; that teachers are teachers in school, not guardians of children's total welfare; that pupils are pupils in school regardless of what other roles may govern their conduct elsewhere;

and that the delivery of group educational services inevitably takes the form of school—a meeting of pupils performing tasks assigned and supervised by a teacher.

Lengthy extracts from original sources have been included to show that the comparisons are direct, not interpreted. The key words and phrases show up in all of the literature. They have become so much a part of the rhetoric of what it means to be an American that successive groups of reformers reproduce the same language, believing the insights to be new. Anyone making choices about schooling will do well to heed the lessons of history in the following pages. It is a history of dedicated people guided by dreams that could not come true.

ACKNOWLEDGMENTS

This book has been written with the encouragement of many friends and colleagues. Six years of teaching elementary school had left me so worn out both emotionally and physically that I had fled into the security of the business world, but all around me I was still hearing complaints about incompetent teachers and inadequate schools. I felt challenged to return to academic pursuits to find answers. What I found was many other people asking the same questions.

I acknowledge with gratitude permissions from Prentice-Hall to quote from Mayhew and Edwards' *The Dewey School*; from Houghton Mifflin Company to quote from Randolph Bourne's *The Gary Schools*; from David Whiting to quote from the Newton schools reports which he courteously supplied to me; and from Jonathan Kozol to quote from his article, "A Junior High That's Like a College."

In addition I am deeply indebted to special individuals upon whom I have imposed more heavily. Arthur W. Foshay and Finette Foshay read and commented on the initial manuscript and helped in other ways far too numerous to list. Hollis L. Caswell's clear insights provided focus when factors to be considered seemed unlimited. Frank G. Jennings read the completed manuscript and provided guidance based on his long experience with publications. Louise Hock read and commented on the revised manuscript, and earlier she had made it possible for me to do the list of curriculum classics included in the appendix. Paul Diederich gave permission to quote from his personal correspondence. Edward J. Meade, Jr. indulged my impositions on the Ford Foundation. Bernard

Everett kindly searched out a mimeographed in-house report long forgotten by others. A. Harry Passow's quiet understanding helped clear up much confusion. Lawrence Cremin's seminar at Teachers College provided invaluable experience. Andrew Conlon advised on the final stages of getting the book printed. Abraham Wilson, my attorney, gave unstintingly of his infinite capacity to solve problems, and Sue Wilson's patience in times of adversity provided a model for emulation. To these people and many others who expressed their concern, my appreciation is heartfelt.

ANGELA E. FRALEY

PART I

THE RHETORIC:

A SEARCH FOR AN IDEAL

1

SCHOOL:

A SOCIAL INSTITUTION

A survey of the literature on school improvement in the United States reveals a pattern of language and action that is apparently re-born with each new generation of school reform philosophers. The labels are different, fine points of semantics are argued, lists of shortcomings are written and rewritten, and purposes of schooling are defined and redefined, expanded and further expanded into rhetoric so all inclusive that the immediate question of schooling becomes lost in the universal question of the meaning of life. From these discussions, the envisioned task of the school becomes that of reshaping human nature. Each new generation produces a few individuals who are willing to try. Again the methods have different labels, but attempts to alter the institution of *school* take the same form, produce the same outcomes, attract the same criticisms, and fade into oblivion as experience teaches each wave of reformers that the task of the total socialization of the child is inappropriate to the school; that the only experiences available in school are social contacts governed by the institution of *school*; and that given the nature of school and the breadth of interpretations possible for the term *democratic*, the designation *democratic school* is a conflict in terms.

The possibilities of arguing this last point are legion. Also

3

legion are the possibilities of having democratic facilities for education without a teacher, but they do not qualify as school. School has a specific task to perform, the teacher is in charge, and the governance is autocratic. It is efficient, and it survives all attempts to alter it. This is not to argue against the desirability of providing democratic educational experiences. It is to argue the illogic of the belief that such experiences can be provided in school effectively. Regardless of the illogic, school reformers traditionally become dedicated to the idea that schools can be youth communities run as miniature democratic societies. When these reformers try to make it happen, they are confronted with an insurmountable confusion of definitions.

Education—Schooling—Experience

Definitions of education unavoidably include consideration of both process and product concerning the social phenomenon of human learning. If learning is education, and living is learning, and awareness is living, and experience is awareness, then all experience is educative in some way, and education as *process* is synonymous with experience. Following on this, if the product of experience is knowledge, then education as *product* is synonymous with knowledge. Thus, the term *education* in its all-inclusive sense, is at best nonfunctional for purposes of discussion. All of this notwithstanding, the term is broadly used and, unless otherwise modified, refers to formal schooling—grammar school, high school, college, and university. The product is a knowledge of reading, writing, and arithmetic and their extensions into fields of specialized study. Only if directly specified does education mean training for a trade, indoctrination in religious ritual, or any of the other societal activities that purposely inform or influence people.

The overall aims of our schooling apparently have not changed since the nation's founding fathers. Schooling is to prepare a population that will function capably as the citizenry of the United States of America—a republic. Beyond the traditional testable function of the school—book learning—is every aspect of experience that does or can contribute to the total socialization of the child. With a blurring of definitions, an imprecise vision of democratic equality is a part of the expected social outcome.

In the days of tutorial instruction for a few children in the home, lessons caused very little disruption of the child's life patterns. With the advent of public institutions of mass schooling for all, institutional regimentation became a major component of the academic learning experience. It is tolerated as a practical adjustment to fiscal economy and societal priorities in the allocation of human resources. The extreme example of this was Joseph Lancaster's monitorial system instituted in New York about 1807. Under Lancaster's plan, one teacher, utilizing cadres of older pupils, supervised basic literacy instruction for classes of sometimes five hundred pupils all in one big room. Although the lessons were heavily regimented and impersonal, it was nevertheless a practical means of giving minimum formal instruction to orphans and the children of the poor who otherwise would have received none. And it qualified as school—a teacher with a room full of children working on reading, writing, and ciphering.

When the terms *education* or *schooling* are used casually, the intended meaning is usually understood in context. Most of the time they are used synonymously. It is generally accepted that certain skills useful for survival in today's society must be systematically learned, and that this is ordinarily most reliably accomplished with the help of a teacher in a school. In this sense, *school* can include every level of formal instruction from institutional day care to university. But, again, unless otherwise specified, the term *school* in America is understood as referring to ordinary schools, public or private, provided for the instruction of normal young people, age five to eighteen. And such is the intended meaning when the terms *school* or *schooling* appear unmodified in the following pages.

The Task of the School

The task of the school is service to pupils, but the term *pupil* denotes a societal role, not an individual. An individual is unique only to himself. To all other people, any individual is a category, the same as all other people are categories to the individual. That is to say, they fulfill societal roles. The only category singly occupied is the category of *self*. Thus, every personal interaction falls into a hierarchy of categories. At school, even when a teacher speaks to an individual pupil, a unique self is receiving the communication in the context of the category *pupil* from the category *teacher*, neither of which category is singly occupied by the individuals involved. If this occurs in a classroom situation, all other pupils in the room occupy the category of *class*. When a teacher speaks to the class as a whole, each one hears as a pupil, but the teacher is speaking to the category *class*. As part of the total school, the pupils disappear into the category *student body*, and outside of the school these individuals are gathered into the categories *children*, or *population*, or any others among infinite possible classifications. Children spend only about thirteen per cent of their time as pupils in school. The rest of their time they are functioning in the context of these other societal categories. So the school is limited to meeting the individual needs only of pupils, not of selves, and this only to the extent that such needs can be determined and that they fall within the functional domain of the category *school*. It is the scope of this functional domain that is ever in question and seems to inspire expectations far beyond human capacity to produce.

School as it exists today has three clear components: the formal curriculum or study tasks, the teacher as framer and dispenser of the study tasks, and the administration as controller of the physical facilities and basic rules of conduct. All of these, of course, are interdependent. The formal curriculum, however, can be thought of as having the most immediacy to the pupils, because pupils are expected to apply themselves to do something with it. This is the reason they go to school. The teacher comes second in immediacy to the pupil, because in a mass education system, the teacher is a technician trained to organize and present the materials of instruction appropriate to a specific group of pupils. The administration comes third in immediacy to the pupil, because apart from assigning pupils to classrooms, it attends to them as a group. It regulates the environment and may well choose the materials of instruction to be made available, but, given the basic uniformity in schools, it is reasonable to view schools as societally controlled, and to view the administration as an agency for the provision of centralized orderly access to the accumulated cultural heritage—at least to as much of it as is commonly useful to members of a given society. The conflict between the philosophical and practical aspects of this last qualification creates the constant controversy about the specific task of the school.

Dissatisfied Observers

In the mid-nineteenth century, the spectacular growth of the nation was taken as proof that democracy was a workable social organization. The difference between a democracy and a republic by definition was, at best, confused in the public mind. A democratic government was thought of as maintaining a society in which every person is free to choose his own occupation and to control his own destiny. The exercise of this freedom logically required that every person have sufficient education to understand and to cope with the duties of citizenship and the provision of his own livelihood, so by 1860 the common schools had come into being. The need for them was backed by the rhetoric of the founding fathers, and it was believed that schools could provide truly democratic educational experiences.

Complaints about the schools have had a familiar ring ever since the common school movement and the compulsory education laws brought the children of the working classes and the immigrant poor into the nation's schools. In 1893, Joseph Mayer Rice's articles in *The Forum* complained about politicians hiring untrained teachers who supervised concert recitations for rote memorization of traditional text material meaningless to most of the children. After spending several months visiting classrooms in thirty-five cities scattered through thirteen eastern and midwestern states, he was moved to write:

The school has been converted into the most dehumanizing institution that I have ever laid eyes upon, each child being treated as if he possessed a memory and the faculty of speech, but no individuality, no sensibilities, no soul.[1]

He had seen classrooms where teachers were "grinding" ready made questions and answers verbatim into the minds of children.[2] In others there were regimented recitations with children bobbing up and down in sequence predetermined by the order of seating. He found restrictions on physical move-

[1] Joseph Mayer Rice, *The Public-School System of the United States* (New York: The Century Company, 1893), p. 31.
[2] Rice, p. 51.

ment, regulating placement of hands and feet and the movement of head and shoulders. He characterized these schools
as subjecting the pupils to "hard, unsympathetic, mechanical
drudgery" and "a discipline of enforced silence, immobility,
and mental passivity." [3] "The innocent child is thrust into
bondage, the years of childhood are converted into years of
slavery," [4] he intoned. The general public came in for its
share of the criticism:

In regard to the public, the mere fact that things are muddled
as they are proves that the citizens take no active interest in the
schools. As for the parents in particular, the fact that they send
their children to unsanitary schools—indeed, so unsanitary as to
be unfit for the habitation of human beings—is of itself sufficient
to prove that they are in no way concerned with what the schools
do with their children. [5]

That same year, the Committee of Ten also took a dim
view of the schools, referring to a:

secondary school course of a very feeble and scrappy nature
[s]tudying a little of many subjects and not much of any one,
getting, perhaps, a little information in a variety of fields, but
nothing which can be called a thorough training. [6]

Remarkably, after seventy years of progressive educators'
attempts to remedy these ills, in 1970 Charles Silberman
visited schools all across the nation and was moved to say, in
synonymous if not identical terms:

I am indignant at the failures of the public schools themselves.
. . . It is not possible to spend any prolonged period visiting

[3] Rice, p. 39.
[4] Rice, p. 95.
[5] Rice, p. 49.
[6] Committee of Ten on Secondary School Studies, *Report* (New York:
Published for the National Education Association by the American Book
Company, 1894), in *Turning Points in American Educational History*, ed. by
David B. Tyack (Waltham, Mass.: Blaisdell Publishing Co., 1967), p. 381.

public school classrooms without being appalled by the mutilation visible everywhere—mutilation of spontaneity, of joy in learning, of pleasure in creating, of sense of self. The public schools . . . are the kind of institution one cannot really dislike until one gets to know them well. Because adults take the schools so much for granted, they fail to appreciate what grim, joyless places most American schools are, how oppressive and petty are the rules by which they are governed, how intellectually sterile and esthetically barren the atmosphere, what an appalling lack of civility obtains on the part of teachers and principals, what contempt they unconsciously display for children as children.[7]

Thus, Silberman attributed it all to mindlessness on the part of educators and of the public in general. He is wrong. It is owing to extreme mindfulness on the part of educators and the public that both Rice and Silberman found a few schools they deemed praiseworthy, conducted presumably in accordance with the principles of democratic freedom for the child. A study of the background of these efforts to produce democratic schooling gives an entirely different perspective.

[7] Charles E. Silberman, *Crisis in the Classroom* (New York: Random House, 1970), p. 10.

2

DEMOCRACY AND EDUCATION: FRANCIS W. PARKER AND JOHN DEWEY, 1883–1903

The Founding Fathers

By 1900, John Dewey was writing dramatically about democracy and education and the need for democratic schools in the United States, but the logic of his rhetoric is rooted deeply in the early struggle for a national character. The commanding presence of the Declaration of Independence and the Constitution predetermines the aims of American public education. Citizens are expected to accept as truths:

that all men are created equal; that they are endowed by their Creator with certain unalienable rights; that among these are life, liberty, and the pursuit of happiness. That, to secure these rights, governments are instituted among men, deriving their just powers from the consent of the governed; that, whenever any form of government becomes destructive of these ends, it is the right of the people to alter or to abolish it, and to institute new government, laying its foundation on such principles, and organizing powers in such form, as to them shall seem most likely to effect their safety and happiness.[1]

[1] *Declaration of Independence*, second paragraph.

Accepting the above, the continuing tasks of the citizenry are:

to form a more perfect union, establish justice, insure domestic tranquility, provide for the common defense, promote the general welfare, and secure the blessings of liberty to ourselves and our posterity.[2]

Acknowledging that power can be perverted to tyranny, Jefferson recommended in 1778 as a preventive:

to illuminate, as far as practicable, the minds of the people at large, and more especially to give them knowledge of those facts, which history exhibiteth, that, possessed thereby of the experience of other ages and countries, they may be able to know ambition under all its shapes, and prompt to exert their natural powers to defeat its purposes.

He expresses faith that a system of free schooling should give basic literacy to all and that selectively, at public expense:

those persons, whom nature hath endowed with genius and virtue, should be rendered by liberal education worthy to receive, and able to guard the sacred deposit of the rights and liberties of their fellow citizens, and that they should be called to that charge without regard to wealth, birth or other accidental condition or circumstance.

He viewed himself as promoting schooling for the purpose of "rendering the people the safe, as they are the ultimate, guardians of their own liberty." [3]

In 1798, Benjamin Rush viewed the establishment of schools at public expense as "laying the foundations for nurseries of wise and good men, to adapt our modes of teaching

[2] *United States Constitution*, preamble.
[3] Thomas Jefferson, "A Bill for the More General Diffusion of Knowledge," and *Notes on the State of Virginia* (1785), quoted in Lawrence A. Cremin, *American Education: The Colonial Experience 1607–1783* (New York: Harper & Row, 1970), pp. 440, 441.

to the peculiar form of our government." He was confident that such schools should "reinforce patriotic prejudice," inspire republican principles as well as duties, encourage "obligations of mutual benevolence," and, as a general and uniform system of education, they should "render the mass of the people more homogeneous and thereby fit them more easily for uniform and peaceable government." He aimed to produce "republican machines." [4] Taken in the context of the times and in the context of lingering regional uncertainties regarding the advantages of a strong federal government, this direct language is more realistic than radical. The ideals had to be celebrated as universal in order to counteract feelings of divisiveness generated by necessary economic adjustments, and to insure that a united strength could be maintained to ward off foreign challenges to independence. In short the prime purpose of education was citizenship education.

The Common School

The arguments that carried the common school movement from 1830 to 1860 echo the words of the founding fathers. Schooling patterned after education for an aristocracy was firmly established in the culture of the educated who saw no reason to change it. This same education was viewed by the workingman as an avenue to social mobility for his children. Thus, there was no argument regarding the desirability of schooling or regarding the basic content. The concern was for extending accessibility and for extending content to accommodate the founding fathers' prescription for

---

[4] Benjamin Rush, "Of the Mode of Education Proper in a Republic" (1798), in *Beaver Island Reprints in the History of Education,* HE#220 (Bergenfield, N.J.: Beaver Island Publishing Co., Inc., 1967), second, third, and fourteenth paragraphs.

the new nation. Preservation of the tradition of social equality was seen as vital while educating for the ordinary duties of American life. These duties commanded informed participation in our republican government, and conduct of personal and public affairs in accordance with democratic ideals tied in with Protestant Christian morality.[5]

Simply, the question in 1830 was not whether children needed education, but what provision would insure that all would be educated. The result was the American common school ideal. It was clearly not enough to provide, at public expense, only pauper schools that would teach the rudiments of literacy to children of the indigent. The accepted simple aim was for a practical understanding among the classes. Promoters of the common school did not expect to do away with social differences, but to provide schooling that would minimize the political effects of class consciousness. As a result, the common school ideal was pounded into shape politically. The demand was for a school publicly supported, publicly controlled, accessible on a free and equal basis to all, and of such high quality that the rich and poor alike would choose to attend it. It was expected to teach intelligent and responsible exercise of citizenship in addition to reading, spelling, writing, and arithmetic for discharge of the ordinary duties of life. The means of doing this had to be "effective in attaining the ends, and republican in their own right," and "it was to provide for the young that which no other institution known to the society could furnish—the experience of democratic association within a genuine miniature of a democratic society." [6]

The common school movement was launched to get the

[5] See Lawrence A. Cremin, *The American Common School: An Historic Conception* (New York: Teachers College, Columbia University, 1951), pp. 28–82.

[6] Cremin, *Common School*, p. 76.

laws passed, the buildings built, and the teachers hired. By 1860, it was at least nominally achieved in every community, and, although quality was certainly irregular, school kept, tuition-free to all, "to be the first stage of training—that stage necessary to all members of the community—from which those who desired could go on to other pursuits, whether in the academic or in the non-academic world." [7]

The public concept of school was uncomplicated. School was school—a teacher and pupils. Moral indoctrination toward ideal democracy was assumed to be the governing orientation. It was expected that traditional studies and proximity in common classrooms, *per se*, would foster not only the needed understanding, but good will among disparately endowed human beings. Robert Dale Owen was among those whose comprehensive view of society prompted him to warn, as early as 1830, that regardless of the ideals taught:

if the children from these state schools are to go every evening, the one to his wealthy parent's soft carpeted drawing room, and the other to its poor father's or widowed mother's comfortless cabin, will they return the next day as friends and equals? He knows little of human nature who thinks they will. [8]

Owen clearly understood the limitations of what could be accomplished in school to counter the economic and political forces that shape social attitudes, but his evaluations in terms of absolutes had little impact on the American public. Human society functions on approximations, not absolutes, so the social interactions within the schools functioned as miniatures not of ideal democracy, but of the humanly flawed society from which the pupils came. The public seemed indisposed to reflect any more deeply on the disparity between the

[7] Cremin, *Common School*, p. 76.
[8] Cremin, *Common School*, p. 39.

ideal and the real. It was left for John Dewey at the turn of the century to question loudly the effectiveness of the teaching and to question whether it qualified as *republican*.

In the meantime, the code of public conduct of the nation was being severely strained. People who had grown up in a simple agrarian society were suddenly faced with social complexity beyond the intellectual grasp of all but a few. And those few commanded money and power that defied imagination. The giant business and industrial trusts were gradually subverting the power of the politician and rendering him subservient to their interests. Whole communities could be deprived of their source of livelihood—their markets, jobs, lands, profits—when pieces of industrial empires changed hands. As each wave of prosperity resulted from excessive exploitation of new industries, panic inevitably ensued—1873, 1893—bringing adversity to almost everyone. With each panic came questions. How had democracy failed? Why was this allowed to happen? With government "of the people, by the people, and for the people," the obvious answer was ignorance on the part of the general population. And since ignorance is presumably remedied by education, each panic brought concentrations of attention to school improvement.

Parker and Dewey

Coincident with the panic of 1873, the Quincy, Massachusetts, school board conducted tests in the schools and found pupil achievement sadly wanting. As a result, Francis W. Parker, full of recent impressions of European school methods, was hired to make changes. The Quincy System attracted national attention, although Parker insisted that there was nothing special or experimental about it—that he had simply adopted the methods used to teach growing children

everywhere except in school. This was the first highly publicized program, for instance, to start the teaching of arithmetic with handling of objects instead of memorizing rules;
to start reading with simple words and sentences rather than
with ab, ac, ad, af, ag, etc.; or to initiate geography with excursions around the countryside instead of memorizing
place names and their latitudes and longitudes.

Parker was evidently a man of intense human sensitivity
and personal modesty. He had thought seriously about the
way children grow and learn. He had traveled in Europe and
observed the work of the early educational theorists. And it
was before G. Stanley Hall's publications on child development, and before the St. Louis and Menomonie manual
training school programs, that Parker put his ideas to the test
in Quincy. By 1883, he was Principal of Cook County Normal School and he based the practice school there on the
same ideas. That year his book, *Talks on Teaching*, was published. At the New York chautauqua in 1891, he gave his
Talks on Pedagogics, elaborating on his ideas which he edited
for publication in 1894. In it he states the beliefs that guided
his work, fully dedicated to the common school ideal:

I believe four things, as I believe in God—that democracy is
the one hope of the world; that democracy without efficient common schools is impossible; that every school in the land should be
made a home and a heaven for children; fourth, that when the
ideal of the public school is realized, "the blood shed by the
blessed martyrs for freedom will not have been shed in vain." . . .[9]

There is but one place where children of all nations and sects
can come together, sit upon the same benches, play upon the
same grounds, live together, work together, *know* each other, and
that is the common school. The principal mission of the common

[9] Francis W. Parker, *Talks on Pedagogics* (New York: E. L. Kellogg & Co.,
1894), p. 451.

school is to dissolve the prejudices that have been inculcated under the methods of oppression.[10]

And Parker had faith that it was going to be achieved:

Already careful investigations in child life are being made by humanity-loving scientists all over the civilized world; wonderful results are at hand.[11]

But he was reaching the end of his career.

Although Parker lived another nine years, it fell to the lot of John Dewey, as an astute social observer and a compulsive writer, to become the synthesizer and chronicler of the innovative educational thinking of his times. Adopting the expository style of the philosopher, he seldom acknowledges sources, and is thus credited with initiating many ideas he picked up from the work of others. It can almost be said that every point in Dewey's later writing on education is made or mentioned in passing by Parker in his two works. One need not even read thoroughly to spot identical vocabulary, even to the "I believe" in Dewey's "My Pedagogic Creed." But Parker said in four sentences what Dewey spread over fourteen pages. Parker's concluding chapter is titled "Democracy and Education," which Dewey later used as a book title. So, by the time Dewey published in 1897, he was talking about things Parker had been saying and doing for twenty-five years. And, although one can compare the works and suspect that Dewey used Parker as an outline, Dewey evidently was never moved to fully acknowledge his debt to Parker. In the Mayhew and Edwards publication in 1936 on the Dewey school, the way Parker's practice school is mentioned can be viewed only as a grudging necessity, owing to the fact that it both preceded and later absorbed and survived the laboratory school. They state that:

[10] Parker, *Pedagogics*, p. 423.
[11] Parker, *Pedagogics*, p. 434.

Both schools were progressive; both had made outstanding contributions to the principles and practice of education. But while
similar in these larger aspects of general purpose, the two schools
differed rather widely in theory, method, and practice.[12]

If this difference existed, it is not revealed in the surviving
reports either of intention or of accomplishments.

It was coincident with the panic of 1893 that John Dewey
was called to head the Department of Psychology, Philosophy, and Education at the University of Chicago. Whatever
may have been his previous thinking on forms of schooling,
when he arrived in Chicago in 1894, he stepped into a fully
established working model of what he subsequently recommended. He entered his son in the first grade of Parker's practice school. A year later he entered his daughter, and a year
after that he opened his own school to which he transferred his
children.

As nearly as can be determined from existing reports, the
Dewey school, if judged by the actual activities and outcomes, differed little from the practice school. The one difference of specific purpose, or organization, was that the practice school was for the training of teachers. The laboratory
school was for the experimental application of Dewey's theories controlled for data gathering, and was eventually departmentalized to facilitate this. Also, the laboratory school maintained a ratio of one teacher for every four pupils—practically
tutorial instruction. The reports do not bear out that there
were measurable differences in methods, materials, or classroom practice. Dewey's view of himself as all wise, and the
steady flow of publications from his pen, undoubtedly gave
his school a reputation for excellence that was only partially
and certainly not uniquely deserved. The school, however,
was unique for the thoroughness of the records made and

[12] Katherine Camp Mayhew and Anna Camp Edwards, *The Dewey School*
(New York: D. Appleton-Century Company, Inc., 1936), p. 13.

preserved, and thus has become the cited example of innovative schooling of its time.

Dewey's steady flow of publications was responsible, also, for giving credibility to the impossible dream of the democratic school that still plagues schools today. The power of his writing to stir the imaginations of idealists captivated by the sentiments of the American democratic ideal has never diminished. The underlying assumption in Dewey's follow-up of Parker's educational philosophy and in the American common school ideal is that there is an identifiable concept of the good life which, given the option, everyone would choose. It assumes further that appropriate schooling of the young could eventually inspire universal choice of this ideal, and that it would result in a social order based on reciprocity of interests and active association amongst members of different societal groups to maintain mutual understanding.[13] Dewey's descriptions of schooling are only apparently directive. They are characterized by impassioned appeals for allowing the child freedom to choose and grow as his natural endowments permit; by negative examples describing the undesirable consequences of existing traditional schooling; and by value-laden adjectives of which all definitions are necessarily subjective, governed by belief, and grounded in variable societal attitudes. Owing to the fact that the structure of Dewey's language conveys an aura of authority that is lost in any restatement, analysis, or synthesis, his elaborations of Parker's work are presented here in direct quotations with comments. They are paralleled with quotations from Parker, because it was the combination of Parker the inventor and Dewey the trumpeter that created the lasting impact.

With reference to the school as a miniature of the greater society, Parker states simply in his 1894 work:

[13] John Dewey, *Democracy and Education* (New York: The Free Press, 1966 [1916]), pp. 85–86.

A school should be a model home, a complete community, and an embryonic democracy.[14]

Dewey, in 1897, states more elaborately:

I believe that the school, as an institution, should simplify existing social life; should reduce it, as it were, to an embryonic form. Existing life is so complex that the child cannot be brought into contact with it without either confusion or distraction; he is either overwhelmed by the multiplicity of activities which are going on, so that he loses his own power of orderly reaction, or he is so stimulated by these various activities that his powers are prematurely called into play and he becomes either unduly specialized or else disintegrated.[15]

Both men reflected the founding fathers' faith in democracy. Parker states that democracy is:

founded upon the principle that society can rule itself; that each member of society contributes to the good of all, lives for all, and receives from all that which all can give. Democracy is the shortest line of resistance to human development. . . . A fundamental principle of democracy is the responsibility of each for all, and all for each. If one is weak, . . . it means the weakness of all. . . .[16]

The foundations of the great American system of education into democracy have been laid by devoted patriots. The people believe in the common school.[17]

Paralleling this, Dewey states his definition of:

a truly democratic society, a society in which all share in useful service and all enjoy a worthy leisure. . . .[18]

A society which makes provision for participation in its good of

[14] Parker, *Pedagogics*, p. 451.
[15] John Dewey, "My Pedagogic Creed," in *The School Journal*, Vol. LIV, No. 3 (January 16, 1897), pp. 77–80, Article II, fifth paragraph.
[16] Parker, *Pedagogics*, p. 419.
[17] Parker, *Pedagogics*, p. 434.
[18] Dewey, *Democracy and Education*, p. 256.

all its members on equal terms and which secures flexible read-justment of its institutions through interaction of the different forms of associated life is in so far democratic. Such a society must have a type of education which gives individuals a personal interest in social relationships and control, and the habits of mind which secure social changes without introducing disorder. . . .[19]

Since a democratic society repudiates the principle of external authority, it must find a substitute in voluntary disposition and interest; these can be created only by education.[20]

And, by education Dewey and Parker meant schooling, but their descriptions of such schooling are far from the structured indoctrination recommended by Rush, and are only apparently directive.

Parker viewed the role of the teacher as a calling to the improvement of humanity and society:

Nothing that is good is too good for the child; no thought too deep; no toil too great; no work too arduous: for the welfare of the child means happier homes, better society, a pure ballot and the perpetuity of republican institutions. . . .[21]

(6) Quality teaching excludes all competition, undue rivalry, and the cultivation of sordid ambition.

(7) The essence of quality teaching is love; its one aim, the truth.[22]

Dewey's similar references to the teacher's role border on religious zealotry:

I believe that the art of thus giving shape to human powers and adapting them to social service, is the supreme art; one calling into its service the best of artists; that no insight, sympathy, tact, executive power, is too great for such service. . . .[23]

I believe, finally, that the teacher is engaged, not simply in the

[19] Dewey, *Democracy and Education*, p. 99.
[20] Dewey, *Democracy and Education*, p. 87.
[21] Parker, *Pedagogics*, p. 451.
[22] Parker, *Pedagogics*, p. 391.
[23] Dewey, "Creed," Article V, tenth paragraph.

training of individuals, but in the formation of the proper social life.

I believe that every teacher should realize the dignity of his calling; that he is a social servant set apart for the maintenance of proper social order and the securing of the right social growth.

I believe that in this way the teacher always is the prophet of the true God and the usherer in of the true kingdom of God.[24]

With this orientation, the task of the teacher looms as infinite. Parker states simply:

(1) The artist teacher watches with the greatest care and assiduity the character of each pupil; watches mental action through all modes of expression. . . .

(3) The artist teacher is everlastingly studying pupils and seeking for better means to assist them in righteous self-effort. Close persistent, indefatigable study of the child and of subjects for the child is a marked indication of the quality teacher.[25]

Dewey enlarges on this idea, characteristically starting with a negative example:

I believe that under existing conditions far too much of the stimulation and control proceeds from the teacher, because of neglect of the idea of the school as a form of social life.

I believe that the teacher's place and work in the school is to be interpreted from this same basis. The teacher is not in the school to impose certain ideas or to form certain habits in the child, but is there as a member of the community to select the influences which shall affect the child and to assist him in properly responding to these influences.[26]

Stressing that children must be led to initiate their own educational activities, Parker states:

[24] Dewey, "Creed," Article V, thirteenth, fourteenth, and fifteenth paragraphs.
[25] Parker, *Pedagogics*, p. 390.
[26] Dewey, "Creed," Article II, thirteenth and fourteenth paragraphs.

Permanent happiness is the result of continuous, persistent self-efforts in the normal, all-sided development of the body, mind, and soul. . . .[27]
education presents the means for the full exercise of the laws of personal development, of which self-activity is the central factor. . . .[28]
A school should be a model home, a complete community and embryonic democracy. How? you ask. Again I answer, by putting into every schoolroom an educated, cultured, trained, devoted, child-loving teacher, a teacher imbued with a knowledge of the science of education, and a zealous, enthusiastic applicant of its principles. . . . Now, let us demand the *artist teacher*, the teacher trained and skilled in the science of education—a genuine leader of little feet. . . .[29]
(5) All quality teaching concentrates in immediate manifestation in character; history lives in the child; civics and ethics mean daily life; science is applied in school and at home. There is no waiting for future effects in quality teaching.[30]

In the same vein, to explain what should happen in school, Dewey states:

Guidance is not external imposition. . . . *It is freeing the life-process for its own most adequate fulfilment.* . . .[31]
It is a development of experience and into experience that is really wanted. And this is impossible save as just that educative medium is provided which will enable the powers and interests that have been selected as valuable to function. . . . The problem of direction is thus the problem of selecting appropriate stimuli for instincts and impulses which it is desired to employ in the gaining of new experience. What new experiences are desirable, and thus what stimuli are needed, it is impossible to tell except

27 Parker, *Pedagogics*, p. 359.
28 Parker, *Pedagogics*, pp. 359–360.
29 Parker, *Pedagogics*, p. 451.
30 Parker, *Pedagogics*, p. 391.
31 John Dewey, *The Child and the Curriculum* (Chicago: University of Chicago Press, 1902), in Martin S. Dworkin, ed., *Dewey on Education* (New York: Teachers College, Columbia University, 1959), p. 102.

as there is some comprehension of the development which is aimed at; except, in a word, as the adult knowledge is drawn upon as revealing the possible career open to the child. . . .[32]

I believe, finally, that education must be conceived as a continuing reconstruction of experience; that the process and goal of education are one and the same thing.[33]

As a guide for the selection of content, Parker says simply:

(2) A course of study is a means to an end; from the course of study the teacher selects that material immediately needed for the advancement of personal mental and moral power. . . .[34]

(4) The artist teacher has some apprehension of the infinity of means directly at hand for the development of pupils.[35]

Tying in these statements, and enlarging on Parker's concept of directed self-activity, Dewey, in his cumbersome style, summarizes his own beliefs with a notable recurrence of vocabulary identical to Parker's:

There is no such thing as sheer self-activity possible—because all activity takes place in a medium, in a situation, and with reference to its conditions. But, again, no such thing as imposition of truth from without, as insertion of truth from without, is possible. All depends upon the activity which the mind itself undergoes in responding to what is presented from without. Now, the value of the formulated wealth of knowledge that makes up the course of study is that it may enable the educator to determine the environment of the child, and thus by indirection to direct. Its primary value, its primary indication, is for the teacher, not for the child. It says to the teacher: Such and such are the capacities, the fulfilments, in truth and beauty and behavior, open to these children. Now see to it that day by day the conditions are

---

[32] Dewey, *Child and the Curriculum*, in Dworkin, p. 102.
[33] Dewey, "Creed," Article II, seventeenth paragraph.
[34] Parker, *Pedagogics*, p. 390.
[35] Parker, *Pedagogics*, p. 391.

such that *their own activities* move inevitably in this direction, toward such culmination of themselves. Let the child's nature fulfil its own destiny, revealed to you in whatever of science and art and industry the world now holds as its own.[36]

If one ignores functional reality, such statements inspire sentiments of full agreement. Problems arise only when attempts are made to use them as referents in evaluations of schooling and teachers. The specific instructional materials to be employed to accomplish these ideals are never designated. The selection is left to the teacher, so the outcome of such schooling is dependent upon teacher talent. Parker seems to have understood this and he ran his school accordingly, encouraging and developing talent in both pupils and teachers. He geared his expectations and the daily activities to what was possible. Dewey apparently never resigned himself to the human limitations, even though his laboratory school, touted as successfully demonstrating the viability of these ideas, was, on all practical counts, a failure.[37] However, the facts of the matter notwithstanding, his pedagogic creed published in 1897 followed by his lectures published as *School and Society* in 1899 "were taken up at once as firmly establishing the worth and practicality of the 'new' idea of education as experimental, child-centered, and directed toward the reformation of society."[38] He continued writing about the laboratory school and about other similar experimental efforts, actually reworking the rhetoric of the common school movement, tying in his astute observations of child develop-

[36] Dewey, *Child and the Curriculum*, in Dworkin, pp. 110–111.

[37] Dewey, himself, wrote in 1936 that "like every human enterprise, the laboratory school came far short of achieving its ideal and putting its controlling ideas into successful operation." quoted in Mayhew and Edwards, *The Dewey School*, p. 7.

[38] Martin S. Dworkin, ed., *Dewey on Education* (New York: Teachers College, Columbia University, 1959), p. 33.

ment, and adding his concept of the interrelationship of democracy and education. Imaginations were inspired. Disciples picked up pieces of his rhetoric and reinterpreted them into rallying cries—inspirational but non-specific as to action—child-centered, the whole child, learning by doing, etc. It started a crusade for democratic schooling that placed a crushing burden on the shoulders of American teachers—responsibility for the total socialization of the child toward the interests of an ideal democracy. Efforts to fulfill the demand abounded.

The Practice School

The practice school was the beneficiary of a lifetime dedicated to the study of pedagogy. Francis Wayland Parker was born October 9, 1837, in Pescataquog, New Hampshire. His ancestry was of enterprising patriots and teachers. A great, great grandfather was a colonel in the French and Indian War; a great grandfather fought in the Revolution; another great grandfather was librarian of Harvard; a grandfather was a teacher, and his mother was a teacher before she married. Parker was destined to live his life constantly on the move, as were many of his generation in the rapidly industrializing nation, and he acquired his education as his curiosity inspired him or as opportunities arose. Apparently highly talented, he entered the village school at age three, already able to read. His father, a cabinet maker, died when the boy was six, so, at age eight, Parker was bonded to a farmer. He continued attending the local school where he had the audacity to stand up in class on one occasion and tell the teacher that he did not know how to teach. At age thirteen, feeling limited intellectually on the farm, he broke his bonds, alienating his family, and worked his way at odd jobs while attending

Mount Vernon Academy in New Hampshire. At age seventeen he obtained his first school of seventy-five pupils. He taught while still attending the Academy, changing to a better paying school each year as his unusual ability to teach became known.

As was tradition in his family, he answered the call to arms in 1861, served four years in the Union Army, campaigned for Lincoln while home on leave recovering from a serious neck wound, and was discharged in 1865 with the rank of colonel at age twenty-seven. He returned to work in the schools, and in spite of constantly clashing with vested interests and local authorities, he became principal of Dayton Normal School and assistant superintendent of the Dayton schools. A five thousand dollar inheritance in 1872 enabled him to go to Germany, complete a two year course in philosophy, history, and pedagogy at King William's University in Berlin, travel Europe visiting schools, and return prepared to prove his convictions about schooling to American educators.

His opportunity was waiting for him. John Quincy Adams and Charles Francis Adams, Jr., on the Quincy school board, surveyed their schools, found them lacking, and invited Parker to make changes. The results were dramatic. The alphabet and conventional textbooks soon faded into the background. Reading, writing, spelling, arithmetic, and drawing became one interrelated study. Starting with an object, the children discussed it, drew it, learned the word written on the chalk board, pronounced it slowly to hear all of the sounds in it, wrote the word on their slates, and when enough words had been learned, made sentences with them. Soon the observations of the geography and history lessons became the subjects of these exercises as did the related scientific inquiries bringing in arithmetic, and the whole curriculum was related. Parker was credited with breathing life, growth, and happiness into the Quincy schoolrooms in just the five years he served as superintendent of schools there.

Invited to Boston in 1880, he spent two years feeling seriously the constraints of New England tradition while on the board of supervisors. Relieved by invitations to both the superintendency of Philadelphia and the principalship of Cook County Normal School near Chicago, he accepted the Normal School at a lesser salary, drawn by the opportunity to train teachers to his ways. It was here, in 1883, that his ideas were set forth in his first book, *Talks on Teaching*. This work outlines his teaching theories. His simple statements and definitions carry the vocabulary that became the slogans of the twentieth century reformers.

Parker adopted from Comenius, "Let things that have to be done be learned by doing them." [39] This became the *learning by doing* slogan almost universally attributed to Dewey, even though Parker refers to it not once but many times. In his discussion of teaching reading, he inserts the reminder, "What I wish to impress upon you is the one pedagogical principle that stands above all others—we learn to do by doing." [40] In his discussion of teaching arithmetic and developing the child's power to work things out for himself, Parker advises:

We learn to do by doing, to hear by hearing, and to think by thinking. . . . The greatest delight of all teaching is to place the difficulty squarely before the pupils (generally by means of objects), and then let them work it out for themselves. If they go wrong, do not tell them they are wrong, but ask the question that will set them right. . . . Lead them to discover, step by step, what you have discovered.[41]

[39] Francis W. Parker, *Talks on Teaching*, reported by Lelia E. Partridge (New York: A. S. Barnes [1883]), p. 18.
[40] Parker, *Teaching*, p. 34.
[41] Parker, *Teaching*, p. 115.

With reference to the child discovering for himself, he further emphasizes that "the knowledge of right comes from leading the mind to discover the truth." [42] These statements are clearly recommending *the discovery method* commonly early attributed to Dewey and later to Jerome Bruner.

Parker adopted from Pestalozzi, "Education is the generation of power." He adopted from Froebel that the true end and aim of all our work is the harmonious growth of the whole being.[43] This became the *education is growth* theme that permeated Dewey's writing, and which, along with the emphasis on the *school as a community*, is the dominant theme in the following quotes from Parker:

A school is a community; community life is indispensable to mental and moral growth. If the act of an individual in any way hinder the best work of the community, he is in the wrong. The highest duty of the individual is to contribute all in his power to the best good of all. This principle is the sure guide to all rules and regulations of a school. How much noise shall there be in the school? Just enough to assist each and all to do their best work. How quiet shall it be? Just quiet enough to assist each and all to do their best work. . . .[44]

The purpose of a school is educative work. By educative work is meant self-effort in the direction of personal development. School order is that state or condition of a school in which the best educative work is done in the most economical manner. The process of education consists in presenting conditions for educative acts on the part of the individual. Method is the special adaptation of educative conditions to individual needs. Teaching is the presentation of conditions for educative self-effort. Training of the body consists in the presentation of conditions which develop the body, and make it a more efficient means of receiving and manifesting thought.[45]

[42] Parker, *Teaching*, p. 167.
[43] Parker, *Teaching*, p. 18.
[44] Parker, *Pedagogics*, p. 337.
[45] Parker, *Pedagogics*, p. 337.

In this last is also reference to *the process of education* which became both the title and the theme of Bruner's reputedly remarkable little book in 1960.[46]

Parker did not believe in tedious tasks just for the sake of teaching self-discipline. He states: "There are plenty of real obstacles that lie in the pathway of human development and progress without the invention of a single artificial one," and to him, the child's time was precious, as the following illustrates:

> I claim two things: first, that there is not one moment to spend upon anything for the mere sake of discipline that has not a practical use in the mind's upbuilding; second, that if the work be adapted to the state of mental and physical power and ability, if every onward movement brings success, if the work be real (that is, upon real things, and not drudgery), then let the child learn to do by doing, for the pleasure of doing and its resultant successes best fits a man to control himself, and master all the difficulties and obstacles that lie before him.[47]

Moral training undergirded everything Parker did. He wrote:

> In all that I have said, and whatever mistakes I have made either in thought or expression, I have had but one motive in my heart, and that is that the dear children of our common country may receive at our hands a development of intellectual, moral, and spiritual power that will enable them to fight life's battle, to be thoughtful, conscientious citizens, and prepare them for all that may come thereafter. Whatever we would have our pupils we must be ourselves.[48]

In Parker's later publication, *Talks on Pedagogics*, the *child centered* school or curriculum, later to become a slogan,

[46] Jerome S. Bruner, *The Process of Education* (Cambridge: Harvard University Press, 1960).

[47] Parker, *Teaching*, p. 161.

[48] Parker, *Teaching*, p. 181.

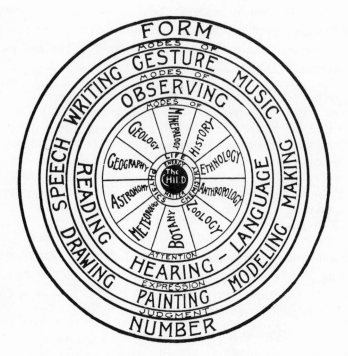

CHART ILLUSTRATING THE THEORY OF CONCENTRATION. *

---

*Parker, *Pedagogics*, p. ii.

is his unifying principle. His chart of what he called the "Theory of Concentration" amounts to a diagram of the child's intellectual universe that would warm the heart of any existentialist. The child is at the center, with the faculties of the mind in concentric circles around it, and the subject disciplines are superimposed as wedge shaped sections of the circle. His emphasis was not, however, on removing all need for the child to conform to society, but on the interrelationship of subject matter in a way that would be meaningful to the child, so that the child's natural interests would lead him to reach out to expand his knowledge in all fields of inquiry, the avenues having been opened by introduction of the disciplines in their elementary form in the child's early years.

Parker had the creativity to view the child's early learning experiences of natural and social phenomena in terms of the subject disciplines that are structured to explain them. He contends that the child functions as an anthropologist throughout its pre-school years; that it begins with the study of its own family life, and extends this study to community life, the neighbors, the children met at play in the house, in the yard, and in the street. Entry into school brings experiences of community control, viewed by Parker as the introduction to the study of civics.[49] Thus, it was but a small step for him to state:

I have urged that all subjects taught in any university shall be begun in an elementary way, with the little child of six years of age, and that exercises in all the modes of expression shall be continued or initiated.[50]

His diagram includes: anthropology, astronomy, botany, ethnology, geography, geology, history, meteorology, min-

[49] Parker, *Pedagogics*, pp. 11–12.
[50] Parker, *Pedagogics*, p. 388.

eralogy, and zoology, all as parts of life, physics, and chemistry. Superimposed in concentric circles, the human faculties to be developed are: 1) modes of attention—observing, hearing language, and reading; 2) modes of expression—gesture, drawing, painting, modeling, making, speech, writing, and music; and 3) modes of judgment—form and number.[51] This was eighty years before Bruner rocked the educational community with "the proposition that the foundations of any subject may be taught to anybody at any age in some form," and that the child could be taught, for example, to approach the study of physics from the point of view of the inquiring physicist, not as textbook material to be learned. In Bruner's words:

Our schools may be wasting precious years by postponing the teaching of many important subjects on the ground that they are too difficult. The reader will find the chapter devoted to this theme introduced by the proposition that the foundations of any subject may be taught to anybody at any age in some form. . . . The basic ideas that lie at the heart of all science and mathematics and the basic themes that give form to life and literature are as simple as they are powerful. To be in command of these basic ideas, to use them effectively, requires a continual deepening of one's understanding of them that comes from learning to use them in progressively more complex forms. It is only when such basic ideas are put in formalized terms as equations or elaborated verbal concepts that they are out of reach of the young child, if he has not first understood them intuitively and had a chance to try them out on his own. . . . A curriculum as it develops should revisit these basic ideas repeatedly, building upon them until the student has grasped the full formal apparatus that goes with them.[52]

Apparently, what was looked upon as revolutionary in 1960 was accepted as simple good sense in 1882. "When offered

[51] Parker, *Pedagogics*, p. ii.
[52] Bruner, *Process of Education*, pp. 12–13.

the principalship of the Normal School, [Parker] saw at once an opportunity both to train teachers and also to work more closely with children themselves—to test out his theories." [53] The facilities that greeted him were anything but ideal, as described:

There was an ill-arranged and dilapidated school building, a dormitory in like condition; no library to speak of, no science laboratories, shops, studios, or gymnasium—very little apparatus of any kind. Confronted by enemies, a hostile press—one hostile both to the school and to training teachers in any way—ignored by the Chicago Board of Education; hampered by the precarious financial support of the school. . . .[54]
The Practice School was indeed poorly housed, and poorly equipped with materials for work. There were too many children in each class room, always from thirty-five to fifty.[55]

Undaunted, Parker set out, as he had in Quincy, to demonstrate that the existing schools, dealing only with subject matter to be memorized and recited, could be changed to miniature democratic communities where the child, as a person, could be inspired to gain the necessary knowledge by self-initiated activities. He organized the teachers and procedures of the school to permit teaching in accordance with his theories, and the task of the school he stated thus:

The conditions must be discovered and applied, by which every child may be developed into the full stature of manhood or womanhood. . . .[56]
The conditions of knowledge and action must be adapted to the development of the whole being. This adaptation, general and individual, is called method, the essential factor in the art of educating.[57]

[53] Ida Cass Heffron, *Francis Wayland Parker* (Los Angeles: Ivan Deach, Jr., Publisher, 1934), pp. 27–28.
[54] Heffron, p. 29.
[55] Heffron, p. 55.
[56] Parker, *Pedagogics*, p. 434.
[57] Parker, *Pedagogics*, p. 434.

Describing the counter-productive consequences of the practices he wished to supplant, Parker lectured:

(1) Methods not adapted to the laws of the being obstruct self-effort, waste the pupil's time, and deprive him of the free use of all his powers.

(2) The learning of dead forms, or symbols without thought, not only wastes the time of children, but cultivates self-conceit, self-consciousness, obstructs the action of imagination, and inhibits reason.

(3) That study of history which demands a belief in the views and prejudices of a narrow-minded author or teacher induces bigotry and hate. History, taught from the standpoint of a creed, a party, or a nation, is often replete with prejudice and false statements. The one-sided teaching of history narrows the sympathies and shuts the soul from the broadest love of humanity.

(4) The text-book study of science, which consists in the verbatim learning of facts that should be gained by observation, and the memorizing of inferences that should be original, hems in a child's spontaneous activities, and robs him of his love for truth.

(5) Drawing from flat copies, and all mere imitations of copies, weakens the power of observation, and reduces the educative influence of art studies.

(6) Corporal punishment degrades the soul, and makes children cowards.

(7) Rewards, marks, prizes, per-cents, cultivate selfishness and destroy unity of action, making the altruistic motive well-nigh impossible.

(8) When a teacher controls by sheer will-power, reinforced by corporal punishment and rewards, his pupils have no opportunity to exercise their own wills.[58]

Parker worked tirelessly, encouraging teachers and improving the facilities of the Normal School and the practice school. Within ten years it was nationally known and was beset with more visitors than it could comfortably handle. He

[58] Parker, *Pedagogics*, pp. 362–363.

had obtained shop and laboratory equipment and a library of over ten thousand volumes for the use of the elementary school pupils as well as the staff and teacher trainees. Visitors were astonished at the happy, industrious children and the feeling of well-being in the school.

The school was planned to function as an interdependent community. Daily opening exercises took place in the assembly hall, conducted by Colonel Parker himself. The program was informal, stressing self-expression on the part of children and adults through the communication of learning experiences. Parker's good will, kindly encouragement, and gentle reminders set the tone. His greeting, "Good morning, ladies and gentlemen," sometimes was followed by, "Am I right?" and his smile scanned the room avoiding a group that had, for instance, been observed snow-balling passers-by that morning. As reported by his biographer:

Questions were often asked from the platform, bearing upon the children's relation to their own homes. "What can you do?" "What did you do after school yesterday?" "What did you do before coming to school this morning?" Repeating the answers, for the benefit of all: "Swept; made the beds; took care of baby brother." "Good," said the Colonel—"Played ball"; again, "Good, anything else?" "Went to the store for mother," was an answer which brought a characteristic comment "That's good—coming to school doesn't amount to much unless it helps you to help father and mother more, and better. That's what real education is. It makes us intelligent and useful." [59]

He often included a reading from the Bible or the reading of a poem from which moral lessons could be drawn. Teachers were encouraged to demonstrate class exercises of special interest; children, individually or in groups were encouraged to

[59] Heffron, p. 67.

report on activities of interest, or to present dramatizations. Class activities provided plenty of material to be communicated. At the close of the assembly, the children reported to their assigned classrooms where the remainder of the day's activities were supervised by the teacher responsible for each group.

Although Parker stressed the child as the center of the learning experience, he certainly had no illusions that the constraints of society could be ignored or could be separated from the subject matter. In the practice school, the society *was* the subject matter, and the specific disciplines were studied for what they contributed to understanding and controlling man's relations to man or to the environment. The materials of instruction were drawn first from the home and the local countryside. Excursions provided specific experiences for nature study and geography. Home activities provided background experiences for chemistry and history. Arts and crafts were ever present in this activity curriculum. The children made drawings of the things they observed, modeled objects in clay, constructed their own laboratory equipment, painted scenery for dramatizations, made relief maps in sand tables, illustrated stories, and composed songs and ballads. The study of reading, writing, spelling, and numbers was a part of every activity. The children created their own stories that were printed in leaflets and used instead of textbooks in the formal reading instruction. They wrote plays and acted them out. They measured, weighed, and calculated results in the science laboratory. They wrote reports to be read before the class. Formal drill was still carried on for these subjects where it was needed, but the content of the materials was always related to the children's current topic of study.

Parker was clear that his methods were designed to stimu-

late the imagination and sharpen the powers of observation.
For example:

> The first steps in geography should give the child the means to
> imagine that which he cannot see. Begin with the forms around
> you; the close and careful study of the chains or ranges of hills,
> valleys, plains, coast-lines, springs, brooks, rivers, ponds, lakes, is-
> lands, and peninsulas. Study them as you do objects in Botany
> or Zoology. Take the children out into the fields and valleys;
> return to the schoolroom; let them describe orally what they have
> seen; then mould and draw it; and, finally, have them describe
> the objects they have seen by writing. Teach them distance by
> actual measurement; boundaries by fences, and other limitations;
> drainage by gutters, and the flow of water after a rain. Let them
> find springs, and discover how the water comes out of the ground.
> Have them bring in different kinds of earth—gravel, sand, clay,
> and loam.[60]

Such activities were to start in the early years, but the formal study of geography was to wait until fifth grade when
they would start with the forms of the continents, moulding
relief maps in sand tables. Then studying the soils led them
into geology, the vegetation into botany, the animals into
zoology. Viewing geography as a study of the earth as the
home of man, these studies brought familiarity with the raw
materials used for food and shelter. This led into study of
the industries required to transform raw materials into items
useful to man, then studies of races of man, governments
and political divisions, cities, commerce, latitude and longi-
tude, all in preparation for history. Stressing that history
must be a study of events of tremendous interest, dates being attached only as they locate events of interest in time,
Parker recommends the use of many books and reference objects, and the development of a school museum. He recom-

[60] Parker, *Teaching*, p. 125.

mends also, analysis of several books with different slants on the same historical event to make pupils aware of authors' biases. If possible, the historical period was to be experienced as here described:

The fourth grade studies Greek history, and the work includes the making of a Greek house, and writing poems about some Greek myth. The children make Greek costumes and wear them every day in the classroom. . . . "They play sculptor and make clay statuettes of their favorite gods and mould figures to illustrate a story. They model Mycenae in sand-pans, ruin it, cover it, and become the excavators who bring its treasures to light again. They write prayers to Dionysius and stories such as they think Orpheus might have sung. They play Greek games and wear Greek costumes, and are continually acting out stories or incidents which please them. To-day as heroes of Troy, they have a battle at recess time with wooden swords and barrel covers. In class time, with prayers and dances and extempore song, they hold a Dionysiac festival. Again, half of them are Athenians and half of them Spartans in a war of words as to which city is more to be desired. Or they are freemen of Athens, replying spiritedly to the haughty Persian message." Besides these daily dramatizations, they write and act for the whole school a little play which illustrates some incident of history that has particularly appealed to them.[61]

Parker's hope, fully dependent upon teacher talent, was that the teacher could view the program as whole, and would be alert to every opportunity for stressing interrelationships, but he expected no miracles. In a way that could be followed by even the most cautious, he suggests:

Indeed, most courses of study, now, involve unification of studies to some extent; geography, for instance, comprehends in a vague way history and most of the sciences. The particular virtue of this theory is that it admits of tentatives. A teacher may

[61] John Dewey, *Schools of To-Morrow* (New York: E. P. Dutton & Company, 1915), pp. 124–125.

see that educative thought has a direct influence over the acts of word-association, and with phonic, phonetic, even word methods, may introduce partially the thought factor in teaching the first steps of reading.

In all text-books on arithmetic there are concessions to the practical use of number in a few of its countless applications to the central subjects; the main line of study may be enhanced by relating arithmetic to geography and science, and the drill work still be continued.

Although copy-book work in penmanship be generally maintained, tentatives may easily be made in the direction of thought expression. A teacher, while following assiduously some "system" of flat copy-drawing, may find occasional place for real drawing in connection with botany, geography, and other central subjects.

In the same line, structural geography may be more effectively coordinated with geology and mineralogy, and history with geography. A glimpse makes way for a gleam, and a gleam broadens into a full blaze of light through honest striving in right directions.[62]

This approach represented a total revision of the role of the teacher. It was no longer one of dispensing information, but of leading children to creative self expression and discovery of truth. By his prescription, a teacher must be educated, cultured, trained, devoted, child-loving, imbued with a knowledge of the science of education, and zealous and enthusiastic in applying its principles. An artist teacher "with light enough ahead to lead, moves on toward truth, hand in hand and heart to heart with the pupil." [63] An artist teacher, in Parker's opinion, will be able to: watch with greatest care and assiduity the character of each pupil; use the course of study as a means to an end, and select from it that material immediately needed for the advancement of personal mental and moral power; study pupils and continuously seek for better means to assist them in righteous self-effort; understand the

[62] Parker, *Pedagogics*, p. 392.
[63] Parker, *Pedagogics*, p. 389.

infinity of means directly at hand for the development of pupils; exclude all competition; exclude undue rivalry; exclude cultivation of sordid ambition; and through love, seek truth.[64]

Parker insisted that the teacher must be prepared with an extensive knowledge of all subjects and the sensitivity to teach them as interrelated, constantly studying and revising the course of study as knowledge increases and society requires different things.[65] He believed that special subject teachers had lost sight of the total, and that only by teaching all of the subjects could a teacher judge accurately all aspects of a child's character and lead him into appropriate pursuits.[66] His teacher training program took all of this into account. Holding that facts must be known before generalizations can be known, he lists: 1) We cannot know which is the better of two methods without knowing both. 2) We cannot know which is best without knowing all. 3) We cannot know any method without knowing the principles which the method applies. 4) One cannot judge a method by seeing it in operation once or twice or without knowing the foundation principles.[67] He insisted that before a trainee was allowed to teach a class, a written paper was required demonstrating a knowledge of the characteristics of the group to be taught, and a complete lesson plan had to be submitted for approval with accompanying instructional materials. Thus, the teaching in the practice school, even by the trainees, was far superior to that found in most schools.

This fact was recognized by the parents in the local community for which the practice school served as the public elementary school. These parents fought for the school through

64 Parker, *Pedagogics*, p. 390.
65 Parker, *Pedagogics*, p. 398.
66 Parker, *Pedagogics*, p. 395.
67 Parker, *Teaching*, p. 16.

all of its political battles. Since the normal school and the practice school were already serving as part of the city system, if only by default, the enterprise was transferred to the city January 1, 1896, and was renamed the Chicago Normal School.[68] This stabilized the situation somewhat, but still did not afford Parker the funding to experiment freely. In 1899 Mrs. Emmons Blaine gathered a group of trustees and created The Chicago Institute Academic and Pedagogic to include a Teachers' Training Department and a Demonstration School with children. The Institute was to have new buildings and a heavy endowment to carry on Parker's work.[69] It was the realization of Parker's lifelong dream, and further recognition was in the offing.

While the Chicago Institute was still housed in temporary quarters, and plans for new buildings were in progress, Parker was prevailed upon to accept an even greater opportunity. At the invitation of President Harper, he and the trustees agreed to incorporate the Institute as the School of Education at the University of Chicago. To provide for the children already attending the temporarily housed Demonstration School on the North Side, Mrs. Blaine endowed a new elementary school to be erected on part of the originally planned site and to be run as a branch of the Demonstration School of the Chicago Institute. This was named the Francis W. Parker School.

The larger enterprise, the Chicago Institute, was to be housed in a beautiful new building which became the Emmons Blaine Hall of the University of Chicago. Parker, however, was destined not to enjoy this particular reward of his long crusade. In February of 1902, before the completion of the new buildings, he complained of being over-tired and was sent to New Orleans to rest. His death on March 2, 1902, left

68 Heffron, p. 32.
69 Heffron, p. 33.

to Dewey the directorship of the new School of Education and the Demonstration School elegantly equipped to put into practice Parker's theories of schooling.[70]

The Laboratory School

By the time Dewey arrived in Chicago in 1894, Parker, his theories, and the practice school had become famous. The school was a working expression of Parker's life and career. The laboratory school, on the contrary, was the product of Dewey's opportunism. Between graduation from the University of Vermont in 1879 and reporting to the University of Chicago in 1894, Dewey acquired a doctorate from Johns Hopkins and twelve and a half years teaching experience—two years in a Pennsylvania high school, a half year in a rural Vermont school, and the rest at the University of Minnesota and the University of Michigan as instructor and then professor of philosophy. He had published *Psychology* in 1887 and *Outline of Ethics* in 1891. Although the department he chaired at Chicago included pedagogy, the schooling of children had not been among his primary interests. He was, however, a participant in study clubs attended by a closely knit group of scholars and educators interested in philosophy and the newly evolving field of psychology. Dewey enlisted the interest of the other parents in this group and started the laboratory school in 1896 as a function of the Department of Pedagogy. Ostensibly "stimulated by a twofold desire for a laboratory to test his educational philosophy and to provide opportunity for growth and development in his own children," he admitted, "it was mainly on account of the children." [71]

[70] Jack K. Campbell, *Colonel Francis W. Parker: The Children's Crusader* (New York: Teachers College Press, Columbia University, 1967), p. 234. And Heffron, pp. 32–34.
[71] quoted in Mayhew and Edwards, p. 446.

A comparative reading of Parker and Dewey substantiates the belief that Dewey started with elaborate restatements of theories adopted full blown from Parker's works, set up his school using Parker's methods and sequence of study topics, kept careful records of small group instruction, and concluded that practice supported his theories. At best, he can be said to have replicated Parker's less formally recorded experimental work. Reports of the activities of the two schools do not support the contention that the laboratory school was much different from the practice school, except that the laboratory school had much smaller classes. Dewey's stated expectation was to:

discover and apply the principles that govern all human development that is truly educative, [and] to utilize the methods by which mankind has collectively and progressively advanced in skill, understanding, and associated life.[72]

To do this, the school was expected to become involved in the work of invention and search rather than resorting to the easy use of existing materials and lessons, and thus make the "difference between inspiring a social outlook and enthusiasm and imposing certain outward social conformities." [73] Certainly this is directly from Parker.

Dewey was emphatic that the laboratory school was not to be thought of as *child centered*, but as *community centered*, to function as a form of community life, a cooperative society on a small scale.[74] However, any such distinction is lost in the following statements of focus:

In planning a school program that was to be an experiment in cooperative living, the child was the person of first concern. There were certain theoretical premises in its underlying hypothesis—

[72] quoted in Mayhew and Edwards, p. 6.
[73] Mayhew and Edwards, p. 468.
[74] Mayhew and Edwards, p. 467.

certain general principles—which were to be aids in understanding its purposes and in guiding its practices.[75]

The primary business of school is to train children in cooperative and mutually helpful living, to foster in them the consciousness of interdependence, and to help them practically in making the adjustments that will carry this spirit into overt deeds. The primary root of all educative activity is in the instinctive, impulsive attitudes and activities of the child. . . . Accordingly, the numberless spontaneous activities of children, plays, games, mimic efforts, even the apparently meaningless motions of infants are capable of educational use, are *the foundation-stones* of educational method.[76]

The problem therefore became one of how to utilize the child's individual tendencies, his original impulses to express himself with such growing power and skill as to help him contribute with increasing effectiveness to the life of his group. For purposes of convenience, these native impulses are roughly classified and described by Dewey under four heads: the social, the constructive, the investigative or experimental, and the expressive. These can all be located on Parker's chart.

In the laboratory school, since teachers were expected to work with the total program in mind and to create a cooperative community, administrative overview was necessary constantly to inform and to organize. When it became clear that one teacher could not provide instruction adequately in all fields in the way Dewey wanted it, departmental teaching evolved—kindergarten, history, science and mathematics, domestic sciences and industries, manual training, art, music, languages, and physical culture.[77] A department head teacher served as investigator, reviewed experimental teaching methods and programs, wrote reports, and furnished material

[75] quoted in Mayhew and Edwards, p. 39.
[76] quoted in Mayhew and Edwards, p. 39.
[77] Mayhew and Edwards, p. 374.

for discussion at weekly faculty meetings. These reports also provided data to Dewey for his Department of Pedagogy researchers.

Using the term *group* instead of *class* or *grade*, distinctions were made between intellectual work and hand-work, and children were loosely grouped by their presumed natural leanings toward one or the other, as well as by compatibility of age and personality. Each group was assigned to a teacher with whom they spent at least half of their time. Pupil leaders were assigned daily by alphabetical order to learn leadership skills. Their experiences in this capacity, however, varied widely depending on the personality of the teacher.[78] For the children there was a set amount of time for active and sitting tasks tailored to each group level. The school day was short, varying from two-and-a-half hours to four-and-a-half hours depending on the age of the children.

To start the day, the children reported to their group teacher under whose direction the previous day's work was reviewed and a program for the current day was discussed and planned. The task of coordinating all of the group's activities with the study topic—called variously: stories, social occupations, history and geography—was the responsibility of this teacher along with the responsibility for their number work. Physical education also met daily, but the other activities—techniques (reading and writing), science, cooking, textile, shop, music, art, excursions, assembly—were scheduled variously one, two, or three times a week, or they might be scheduled for alternate quarters, or successively for a month of cooking, a month of textile, and a month of shop, for instance. Approximate allocations of pupil time were: fifty per cent social occupations, ten per cent physical education, ten per cent divided between art and music, and thirty per cent for irregularly scheduled hand work, active work con-

[78] Mayhew and Edwards, p. 377.

nected with the social occupations study, assembly, and any individual drill work needed on reading and writing skills which could preempt time from the other activities.

The curriculum content was to be selected as a continuation of life outside the school, and mental development was expected to come about as a product of social participation. Activities were to be carefully recorded and evaluated to discover:

those things which are genuinely personal experiences but which lead out into the future and into a wider and more controlled range of interests and purposes.[79]

Dewey lamented that custom and convention tend to conceal the intellectual poverty of the traditional course of study—that "much school material is irrelevant to the experience of those taught," [80] and that school subjects exist only in school and are not organized into relationships.[81] In an attempt to select subject matter which could function as organic parts of present social needs of children, with children and teachers sharing emotionally, practically, and intellectually,[82] the prescribed curriculum of the laboratory school was centered around occupations, not studies. Beginning with the occupations of the home, the activities turned to occupations outside the home—the larger social industries of farming, mining, and lumbering. The materials, products, and means of production provided content for scientific inquiry and experiments and also for historic research into the development of industry and inventions.

The laboratory school pupils were thus scheduled into such fundamental activities of humanity as cooking, weaving, car-

79 Mayhew and Edwards, p. 469.
80 Mayhew and Edwards, p. 469.
81 Mayhew and Edwards, p. 468.
82 Mayhew and Edwards, p. 472.

pentry, pottery making, and sewing.[83] Although they were under close supervision, the children were expected to experience from these activities the joy of creation and the exercise of foresight, planning, retrospective reviews, and the need for further information and insight into the principles of connection or interrelatedness of all of these activities. These activities, coincidentally, were presumed to instill the habits of self-induced patience, perseverance, and thoroughness.[84] They were further expected to stimulate the felt need for scientific investigation—into heat and water, for instance, as a result of cooking; or into telephones, electricity, and clocks as a result of studying industrial development and invention. During this activity work, pupils were to be guided through an awareness and discussion of each phase. For example, planning the shape of pottery depending on the intended use, making it, using it, assessing the flaws, and making another better. One group worked with photography, another group built a clubhouse.[85]

Although the actual subjects of study were presumably chosen with the participation of the immediate group of *children*, the prescribed sequence of topics within which the selections were to be made was: primitive life, world wide explorations and discoveries, Chicago and the Virginia and Massachusetts Bay colonies, the union of the colonies and the revolution, American history from the European point of view, the structure and function of the Constitution, the acquisition of new territory, westward expansion and industrial development to 1830, review of history or study of Roman history, and chronological order of the development of civilization. Apparently the *teachers* were expected to set the tasks, at least the topic and method of approach. The pupils

[83] Mayhew and Edwards, p. 473.

[84] Mayhew and Edwards, p. 5.

[85] Mayhew and Edwards, p. 378.

were expected to perform experiments or delve into reference materials that opened up the possibilities for enlarging experience. The refinement of reading, writing, and number skills was expected to grow out of the needs and results of activities. It was assumed that participating in social occupations related those engaged in them to the basic needs of developing life, and thus demanded cooperation, division of work, and constant intellectual exchange by means of mutual communication and record.

A highly sensitive or highly *autocratic* administration was implicit to maintain the great flexibility of organization required to keep problems solved and the program moving productively.

Recommended methods show up clearly in the following description of a year's program for eight-year-olds:

> The Phoenicians were finally chosen for the study of this year because the fixed habitat of this people was similar to the imaginary location of the tribe of metal workers of the previous year, and yet presented conditions that were different from and unfavorable to the earlier life experience of the tribe, up to this time a nomadic pastoral people living on a plain beyond the mountains. . . .[86]
>
> For a tribe of people like the Phoenicians, with the sea in front and mountains behind, agriculture and flocks and herds were impossible as a means of support. The conditions had to yield a means of subsistence, however, if this tribe were to continue. How this could be done was the first problem given to the children.[87]

Presumably from discussion, dramatization, and creative problem solving, the children confronted and experienced the development of fishing, timber, and metal trades carried on with other tribes in exchange for wheat or wool. They met

[86] Mayhew and Edwards, p. 118.
[87] Mayhew and Edwards, p. 119.

the problems of barter, the making of articles to exchange for things they could not produce, and they recognized the function of sailors as middle men. This worked into the question of record keeping and the need for written language and counting: first, pictures and tallies, then the length of the forearm as the cubit, then establishing a standard and the use of sticks of the same length:

The next most apparent need was a unit of weight. In group discussion they decided that water would make the most convenient and common thing to use and talked over ways and means of making a standard. Each child finally made and paraffined a square box the size of his smallest linear unit—the distance from the tip of the thumb to the first joint. This was filled with water, weighed, and taken as the standard unit of weight.[88]

This led into construction of scales and measures used today, and the construction of an alphabet using parts of pictures to make letters. Then they made up stories of imaginary events, and mapped the territory in a sand table as here described:

The high rock coast with its stretch of shore along the sea was planned and built; lead and iron ore were cleverly hidden in the clefts of the mountains to be discovered later; and miniature forests of oak, pine, and other trees were set up for the forests. The aid of the art teacher was sought. . . .[89]

The sort of houses that they as a Phoenician tribe should build was discussed, and it was decided that stone might be used, since there was such an abundance. The question of how it could be made to stick together was brought up and led to a discussion of lime in its native state and its use as mortar. The children then turned into masons, made mortar boxes, trowels, and a sand sieve in the shop. Lime was procured, and experiments were carried on to demonstrate the effect of water upon it. Mortar was made and used to build the walls of a typical house of that time and re-

[88] Mayhew and Edwards, p. 121.
[89] Mayhew and Edwards, p. 123.

gion. A bridge was necessary to cross a ravine; bricks were made from clay; and the bridge built in the form of a keystone arch.[90]

The need to get the walls straight introduced the need for a plumb, which moved into an investigation of gravity, air currents, water flow, water wheels for power, and windmills.[91] It is mentioned here that in another year under another teacher, the study included an imaginary migration (by the class) to Greece, where a highly different civilization from the Phoenician was in progress.[92]

This method of teaching presumably accomplished the following essentials:

First, that the pupil (or research worker) have a genuine situation of experience—that there be a continuous activity in which he is interested for its own sake; secondly, that a genuine problem develop within this situation as a stimulus to thought; third, that he possess the information and make the observations needed to deal with it; fourth, that suggested solutions occur to him which he shall be responsible for developing in an orderly way; fifth, that he have opportunity and occasion to test his ideas by application, to make their meaning clear, and to discover for himself their validity.[93]

The activities as described seem quite exciting, but it is open to question how much was actually initiated by the children, how much time was spent on the projects, who found time and money to procure materials (i.e., enough stone, lime, and equipment to build the walls of a house), and how expertly the projects were carried out. Also, if indeed the English, history, science, mathematics, art, music, and shop teachers coordinated such studies for what must have been ten or more groups of children, the school prop-

[90] Mayhew and Edwards, p. 123.
[91] Mayhew and Edwards, pp. 123–125.
[92] Mayhew and Edwards, p. 125.
[93] Mayhew and Edwards, p. 140.

erty would soon have been a jumble of stone houses, Roman roads, water wheels, wheat fields, etc., unless these were all table models of such things. Dewey probably never had to confront this problem, since the school existed for only eight years, successively in four different locations.

The emphasis was on group work, and there was much reference to classes meeting in the several subjects; however, with a pupil-teacher ratio of about four to one, the basic skills instruction must have nearly approximated a tutorial. The content of the instruction in the basic subjects apparently differed little from conventional schooling. The differences were mainly in the extra attention given to the planning and presentation of lessons, and in the addition of the activity or construction aspects of the learning experiences which made much heavier demands on teachers and the school plant.

The teachers in the laboratory school were expected to perform as gentle catalysts to pupil learning—guides and leaders, to provide what the child needed to carry out self-initiated activity,[94] no longer to assign lessons and listen to recitations. The teaching task was thus redefined. Application of Dewey's principles was in the hands of the teachers for development and modification of methods.[95] The development of concrete materials was also the responsibility of teachers.[96] Constant conferences were necessary to maintain unity in the program, and teachers were selected for fitness to adopt new ways and willingness to assume extra responsibility in emergencies. Faculty meetings, conducted by Dewey, became seminars in method.

It proved not to be easy for teachers to hit upon proper methods of leadership in cooperative classroom activities.[97]

[94] Mayhew and Edwards, p. 375.
[95] Mayhew and Edwards, p. 365.
[96] Mayhew and Edwards, p. 367.
[97] Mayhew and Edwards, p. 468.

Mayhew and Edwards admit that the laboratory school imposed upon teachers, if anything, too much responsibility over all, and too little assistance either in advance or as critical evaluation.[98] They also report that:

when manual training, art, science, and literature were all taught, it was found that one person *could not* be competent in all directions even if this had been desirable.[99]

Since Dewey had absolute control of the school and complete cooperation of parents who were willing to have everything his way, reports of success must be accepted with caution. There were those who were unimpressed.

Consolidation

In 1902 when the School of Education was established with Parker's heavily endowed Chicago Institute as its nucleus, adjustments were bound to come. The University found itself possessing, not only a separate department of pedagogy now more properly a part of the School of Education, but also it had two elementary schools. One, a practice school for the training of teachers, was heavily endowed. The other, the laboratory school of the University's Department of Pedagogy directed by Dewey, primarily an exclusive school for children of the university community, had no endowment. Parker's death in March of 1902 speeded the consolidation. Dewey accepted the directorship of the School of Education and arranged to move the laboratory school into the new building, apparently assuming that the regular teaching and administrative staff of the school would become a part of the School of Education, and that they would be

98 Mayhew and Edwards, p. 366.
99 Mayhew and Edwards, p. 377.

retained indefinitely at his discretion. "The School of Education then became the united faculties, students, and administration of four schools, The Chicago Institute, The Chicago Manual Training School, The University of Chicago Laboratory School, and the South Side Academy." [100] But further changes were coming. Dewey was informed the following spring that by prior arrangement with the trustees of the Chicago Institute, certain members of the administrative staff of the laboratory school were to be eliminated at the close of the first year, among them Mrs. Dewey as principal. Unable to accept this, Dewey immediately resigned, first as Director of the School of Education and shortly after as Head of the Departments of Philosophy, Psychology, and Pedagogy.[101] His children had outgrown the school, and the solution of its problems was no longer of personal importance to him. He moved to New York to join the Department of Philosophy at Columbia University.

The activities of the laboratory school paralleled those of the practice school far more than they deviated from them. Dewey's seeming extension of the ideas into many more areas of concern stressing the cooperative community and social reform add up only to more elaborate statements of what Parker accepted as given. The attitudes toward the children were the same, and the guidelines for choice of activities and subject content were the same. It is even possible that the children in Parker's practice school had a more immediate experience of the give and take imposed by community pressures than did the children in Dewey's laboratory school where there was sufficient staff for tutorial instruction. Both of the schools had vital activity programs. Dewey may well have believed that he could communicate the theories more

[100] Mayhew and Edwards, p. 14.
[101] Mayhew and Edwards, p. 18.

precisely and demonstrate a more completely controlled practice, but, by his own later admission in 1936, the laboratory school "came far short of achieving its ideals." [102] His *Democracy and Education* in 1916 made no point of practical limitations. Such matters were, by omission, relegated to the domain of the teacher.

[102] quoted in Mayhew and Edwards, p. 7.

3

DEMOCRATIC FREEDOM OF CHOICE IN WORK–STUDY–PLAY SCHOOLS: THE GARY PLAN, 1908–1938

Certainly at a time when science and industry were accomplishing previously impossible feats, the decision to provide what was, in effect, freedom of choice in a school must have appeared to be comparatively uncomplicated. As a result, the impracticability of Dewey's recommendations was ignored by most of his followers, but in the hands of William Wirt, the schools of Gary, Indiana became an example of what *could* be done toward accomplishing the ideals.

Although he was a proponent of Dewey's philosophy, William Wirt was not a dreamer. Parker and Dewey had started with the child, and, through supervised excursions and individual attention from highly talented teachers, they extended the child's reach out of the school and into the real world for learning experiences. Wirt was faced with a public school system that afforded him only one teacher for every forty pupils. He could offer neither individual attention nor supervised excursions tailored to small group needs, so he resorted to the reverse strategy of bringing the experience opportunities within reach in a way that children could choose for themselves.

In Gary, Indiana

Wirt arrived in Gary, Indiana, in 1908 to organize a school system that would meet the needs of a predominantly immigrant working class population which was doubling each year with the growth of the steel industry. Eight years of experimenting with what he called work-study-play schools in Bluffton had convinced him of the viability of his two fixed principles:

First: All children should be busy all day long at work, study, and play under right conditions.

Second: Cities can finance an adequate work-study-and-play program only when all the facilities of the entire community for the work, study, and play of children are properly coordinated with the school, the coordinating agent, so that all facilities supplement one another and "peak loads" are avoided by keeping all facilities of the school plant in use all of the time.[1]

His school system at Gary was a direct attempt to provide an environment in which all could have access to the variety of activities recommended by Dewey. In setting priorities, Wirt reasoned, "if the school is to educate the whole child, the first need is evidently a place for him to grow." [2] This meant to Wirt not only classrooms for traditional school subjects, but also special drawing and music studios, workshops, laboratories, libraries, auditoriums, gymnasiums, play fields, gardens, swimming pools, museums, art galleries—in short, opportunity for supervised exposure to all of the aspects of community cultural living such that a child could pursue in-

[1] Randolph S. Bourne, *The Gary Schools* (New York: Houghton Mifflin Company, 1916), p. vii.
[2] Bourne, p. 19.

terests and test his own capacity to participate. Providing this accessibility is primarily a problem of administration. Only secondarily and by default is it a component of creative teaching. So Wirt tackled the administrator's job.

First, he refurbished the existing school by restoring the auditorium that had been partitioned into classrooms, converting the spacious attic into a gymnasium, transforming half of the classrooms into arts studios and laboratories, building an all-trades workshop around the engine room in the cellar, building a domestic science room in an unused corner, putting lockers into previously wasted space, and equipping the playground with apparatus.[3]

Second, and almost immediately, he planned and built two new schools, Emerson and Froebel, incorporating the ideal facilities. Bourne describes them:

The ideal Wirt school plant, such as the Emerson School in Gary, in its open space of ten acres, besides its playground filled with apparatus, has gardens, tennis courts, ball fields, running tracks, and handball courts. For the younger children there are wading-pools, and sandpits. One field is arranged so that it may be flooded in winter for skating. There are two acres of school-gardens, and a cluster of cages and houses for the animals of the school zoo. . . .

The Emerson School has two gymnasiums, one for boys and one for girls. It has also a large swimming-pool. The Froebel School has two gymnasiums and two swimming-pools. . . . It is intended to build pergolas about the inner court which will contain open-air classrooms and additional outdoor gymnasium space. . . .

The school building is built around a great court, with broad halls as wide as streets, and well lighted from the court. These broad halls serve not only as the school streets for the constant passage of the children between their work, but also as centers for the "application" work, or for informal study. They are so

[3] Bourne, p. 33.

wide that all confusion is avoided. . . . The beginning of an art gallery has been made [in the corridors]. . . .

The school museum is an essential feature of the Wirt school . . . so that the children can know the treasures and live with them and learn about them. . . .

In both the Emerson and Froebel Schools there is a branch of the public library, under a library assistant. Children use the library as a part of their regular work. . . .

Few schools have assembly rooms like that in the Froebel School in Gary, with its stage large enough for a full-sized basketball game or athletic contest. . . .

[In the classrooms] many of the lower grades have a desk, made in the school, which is a kind of workbench. These desks have vises attached, and loose tops, which can be readily replaced when soiled or worn out. The seat is a four-legged stool, which can be pushed out of the way when the child is using his desk for a workbench. On occasion the children can take up their stools and desk tops and go off to work in the halls or garden. . . . In the history room . . . are broad tables that can be used for map-drawing. . . . [It] is a real history laboratory. Maps and charts made by the pupils cover the walls, magazines lie about, pictures and books overflow the tables. . . . [It is a] room saturated with history, past and present. . . .

Music and expression and drawing are taught, not in regular classrooms, but in special studios, . . . equipped with all the facilities to impress upon the child with what seriousness these things are taken in the Wirt school. . . .

The science laboratories . . . are workshops as well. The botany room . . . has a large conservatory of vines and plants at the end; the zoology room has a menagerie of small pets, fowls and birds, guinea-pigs and rabbits. The physics rooms are in contact with a machine room where automobiles and other machines illustrate the practical application of scientific principles. . . .

The manual and industrial work is, of course, an essential feature of the Wirt school. The shops are much more extensive than is customary in even the most progressive public school, or even in the special trade school. The Emerson School in Gary has, for instance, a carpentry-shop, cabinet-shop, paint-shop, foundry, forge, machine-shop, printery, sheet-metal shop, electrical shop, sewing-room, and cooking- and dining-rooms, all admirably equipped as regular shops, and not merely as manual-training rooms. The Froebel School has, besides these shops, a plumbing-shop, a laundry, a shoemaking-shop and a pottery-shop.

When we have mentioned the room for commercial studies, the supply-store, the kindergartens and nurseries, the draughting-rooms, indoor playrooms, teachers' room, conservatory, doctor's room and dental clinic, offices, etc., our survey of the school plant is complete. The arrangement of rooms itself, however, is very significant. As we pass around the second floor of the Froebel School, for instance, we meet, in this order, pottery-shop, laundry, freehand drawing-room, two classrooms, physics laboratory, music and expression studios, conservatory, two classrooms, botany laboratory, and four more classrooms. . . . All the rooms, moreover have glass doors, and the shops have windows, so that the children, passing through the halls, may look in and see others at work at unfamiliar tasks.[4]

By applying the principles of scientific management, Wirt was able to finance all of the extra facilities at a lower cost per child than was ordinarily expected for a simple classroom building. He also paid the highest teacher salaries in the state. Adjusting to the practical demands of coordinating the school program, he hired a curriculum supervisor, had special "application" teachers in the auditorium and shops to handle the activity and construction aspects of study projects, used older pupils as teacher assistants, allowed conferences and work on projects to overflow into the spacious corridors, set up cooperative teaching arrangements where it seemed advantageous, and assigned each teacher as "register teacher" for a specific group of children for the purpose of knowing and adjusting to unusual family circumstances.

In accordance with his fixed principles, Wirt lengthened the school day. School was in daily session from 8:15 a.m. to 4:15 p.m. for all children, nursery school through grade

[4] Bourne, pp. 23–31.

twelve, in the same school. He thus kept *all children busy all day long at work, study, and play under right conditions.* The lengthened school day provided more time for special activities without reducing the time spent on regular studies, and it allowed for utilizing pupil work productively in the operation of the school community. Having the total program for all ages in the same school buildings gave the younger children access to the workshops, laboratories, swimming pools, instruction from specialists, etc., ordinarily available only in high schools. Work in the shops and laboratories could be viewed from the corridors through windows, arousing the curiosity of other children, and younger children were permitted in the shops to watch or to serve as helpers for the older pupils who were working. This helper and observer system made for a cooperative rather than a competitive spirit in work, and children and teachers alike learned from watching and asking questions—the most natural way. Having the total program in the same school also did away with the usual breaks in the educational continuity. There was no completion until grade twelve. There was simply more of interest and value to learn, and the dropout rate was measurably lower than that for working class children in other cities.

The pupils were divided into two groups alternating use of the facilities, a practice that came to be known as the *platoon* plan. When group X was in classrooms, group Y was in gymnasium, auditorium, laboratory, etc. School was in session all year divided into four quarters. By these arrangements, *all facilities of the school plant were kept in use all of the time and supplemented one another.* Each group was scheduled to spend half of the morning and half of the afternoon in classrooms, and the other half of their respective schedules was spent in the active work areas. The alternation of academic and activity periods served to reduce problems of fatigue for both pupils and teachers. Also, two teachers shared a classroom on an alternating schedule throughout the day. Teaching was departmental, and classes were rotated so that teachers could render the greatest service with the least expenditure of energy, and the room could be arranged to stimulate in the children an appreciation of the whole scope of the subject being taught.

During the day, the pupil had three sixty-minute periods given over to academic work; one or two sixty-minute periods, depending upon his grade level and program, to physical education and play; and one sixty-minute period to auditorium and one or two sixty-minute periods to special activities. The simple fact that all of the children were not sitting in classrooms at the same time allowed for a flexibility of scheduling that could accommodate any type of special need as well as the full range of normal needs of children. Pupils could do work in different grades in different subjects. The handicapped, or children with frail health, could be scheduled into a full day of school in whatever activities their capacities permitted or which the school health advisors prescribed.

There was a provision for release time *to coordinate the facilities of the entire community for the work, study, and play of children.* At the request of parents, children could be scheduled to attend special activities outside the school, such as religious instruction or music lessons. In cooperation with the factories, there were work-study programs so that pupils who needed to start gainful employment early could continue their schooling.

Since the Gary schools provided both physical facilities and skilled instructors for the extension of basic learnings into practical applications or formal group communication, teachers had to adjust to a different relationship to one another as well as to the pupils. This demanded, of teachers, more initiative and the assumption of heavier responsibility to community feeling in the school, but they all had the advantage of being specialist teachers, even in the elementary grades. They were expected to be guide and mentor to the pupils in line with Dewey's philosophy, but after the practical pattern of Montessori. Room assignments were arranged so that an inexperienced teacher was assigned to share with an experienced teacher who performed a low-key teacher training function. Although instruction in the classrooms was left to the choice of the teacher and usually followed conventional forms, teachers were expected to cooperate on the program for each class, planning together for the application work which took on an interdisciplinary character.

All of the subject teachers were expected to include specific instruction in basic language and mathematics skills appropriate to work in their specialty such as spelling tests in physics or history classes, practical mathematics along with shop instruction, and the essentials of good composition in written reports in any subject. The playground and gymnasium teachers were expected to conduct physical education programs that carried out the recommendations of the school health education advisors, and the auditorium teachers coordinated their programs for each group with the application recommendations of the classroom teachers. The shop teachers were actually skilled artisans charged with teaching the shop techniques while using the maintenance and repair of the grounds and buildings as a textbook. They also supervised the construction of apparatus for science experiments or whatever was needed for application work from any of the other classes in cooperation with the specialty teachers.

The information pamphlet sent to job applicants stated bluntly:

Any person who is not willing to throw himself whole heartedly into this work, who does not desire hard work, who does not

believe that the school is a social institution extending its activities into the community, and who is not particularly interested
in the social welfare of its boys and girls should not apply.[5]

Graduation from an approved normal school was required for
all elementary teachers. High school teachers were required
to have a degree from a four year college in the specialty to
be taught. All were required to have Indiana teaching licenses.

Learning by doing was the keynote of the Gary instruction.[6] Character training occurred as a by-product. "Self-
activity, self or cooperative instruction, freedom of movement, *camaraderie* with teachers, interesting and varied work,
study, and play, a sense of what the school is doing, social in-
trospection, all combined . . ." to cultivate desirable intellectual qualities and self-reliance.[7] Under Wirt's administration, *school* was to be the place where children wanted to be
—as open to them as the public streets. Each child's place at
school was not a desk and chair, but a locker and the spacious
corridors through which the children moved freely in pursuing their scheduled activities or individual interests.

There were two divisions of studies at Gary:

1. Regular work included: reading, language, spelling, writing, arithmetic, geography, history, auditorium, and physical
training. Apparently the instruction in these courses differed
little from traditional schooling except that the teachers coordinated the content to coincide with the subject being
studied in the history class. The *learning by doing* focus was
accommodated with a provision for application or expression work as part of each subject studied. This took the form
of constructing relief maps in sand tables for geography, using the machine shops to construct scientific equipment,

[5] Gary, Indiana, Board of Education, *Information Concerning Work-Study-Play Schools.* Circular of Information to Applicants for Teaching Positions (Gary: Board of Education, 1925–1926), n.p.

[6] Bourne, p. 96.

[7] Bourne, p. 142.

using the chemistry laboratories to analyze foods, using the print shop to publish reports of class or school projects, using auditorium time to work out and present original dramatizations on topics referred to the auditorium teachers for specific groups by subject teachers.

2. Special work included: handwork, freehand drawing, mechanical drawing, nature study, science, music, expression, application, manual training, shop work, and household arts. A broad, interrelated view of nature study and science brought in, as needed, zoology, botany, physics, and chemistry. Library was a course of instruction, and there was an orchestra. The projects in expression and application were topical in character and used the appropriate materials from the immediate environment as the focus of studies.

The physics classes used the lighting, heating, and ventilating systems of the school as a textbook. Along with investigating the function of the equipment and maintaining it, pupils studied the different types of thermometers and the internal structure of meters for electricity, gas, and water. They investigated the weight and density of the air, the moisture in substances, and the function of the bicycle and the automobile.

The work in chemistry included testing the quality of the coal and cement delivered to the school, a study of starch conversion and fermentation as an extension of learnings in the cooking class, testing the dyes used in commercial jellies, testing the tap water, testing foods delivered to the school cafeteria, and testing candy sold at a nearby store. One group used forms from the city inspector's office and did a bacterialogical examination of the milk from several local dairies.

The zoology pupils used both a textbook and the laboratory. They studied, for instance, the relationship of insects to human disease, and the ecological relationships of insects, animals, and plants. These pupils also took part in caring for an on-going project in poultry raising from incubator to market, and in caring for the animals in the school zoo.

The botany pupils took care of the garden, the shrubbery on the school grounds, and the potted plants in the school green house and corridors. In connection with this, they made outlines of soils and plants, they made charts of plant reproduction, studied farm crops and dangerous plants, and in the process learned to use a microscope.

The cooking classes ran the school hot lunch program, accounting pupils took care of the supply room and, under guidance, worked in the school office. Carried on as the application aspects of classwork, these activities utilized the extra time in the lengthened school day, and in no way detracted from the academic programs of the pupils or the school.

Many of these activities were organized into auditorium presentations by groups or individuals. There were reports, debates, dramatizations, or, as in one case, a boy exhibited two mallard ducks he had mounted himself, and gave a lecture on the life history of mallards.[8] The auditorium period had three parts. Half of the period was devoted to music, and the other half to other types of presentations, with a five minute period of marching in between.

In the shops, under skilled instructors, exercises in method were applied to useful production for the school. The equipment was superior to that found in many vocational training schools. The pupils benefitted three ways: from learning the skills, from the experience of completing a job, and from the satisfaction of seeing their products in use by the school community. In addition, once the skills were learned, pupils had free access to the shops to make anything they wanted for themselves.

The fact that the children were producing useful items

8 Abraham Flexner and Frank P. Bachman, *The Gary Schools: A General Account*, Part I (New York: General Education Board, 1918), pp. 112–116.

inspired them. The pupils in the machine shop made drilling pipes for soap retainers, lock castings, woodworkers' bench vises, and printing chases. They repaired seats, an arc lamp, an emery grinder, and a model locomotive.[9] In the forge, pupils made damper rods for furnaces, iron brackets for shelves, stencil knives, and stairway railings. In the foundry, they made castings for playground equipment, automatic locks, lathes, and pump valves. In the print shop, the pupils produced report and record blanks, program schedules, transfer cards, excuse blanks, deposit slips, letterheads, and envelopes as well as publications for the school. In the cabinet making shop they made window brackets, building blocks, and Montessori sets. They filled an order for thirty teachers' desks, and did various repairs around the buildings. In the sheet metal shop, the pupils made dust pans, desk trays, water buckets, paper trays, mail boxes, and light reflectors. Pupils in the plumbing shop installed sinks, basins, and shower baths, and took care of repairing drains and faucets. The painting shop refurbished outside sashes and frames, repainted classrooms, shellacked building blocks, and took care of oiling the gymnasium floor. The shoe repair shop provided facilities and instruction for the children to repair their own shoes or those of members of their families. At Jefferson, the industrial arts pupils ran the heat and power plant, built bookshelves, built cupboards for the shop, and built the tool room.

It is reasonable to conclude from these reports that the Gary plan produced not a school, but an institution that brought a full range of cultural experiences within reach of children. Bourne described it as fully successful:

We may sum up the Gary school, then, as primarily a school community for children of all ages between nursery and college,

9 Flexner and Bachman, p. 130.

providing wholesome activities under a fourfold division of work, study, play, and expression. It aims to provide the best possible environment for the growing child throughout the course of a full eight-hour day. The school community, replacing the old-time education of household and school, aims to be as self-sustaining as possible, all activities contributing to the welfare of the school community life. By the multiple use of school facilities, on the plan of public-service principles, such a school may be provided at no more expense than that of the ordinary public school. The economics effected by this multiple use enable the Gary school to provide recreational and educational facilities for adults as well as children all the year round, as well as to pay better salaries to teachers, and completely solve "part-time problems." It makes the school the cultural center of a community with parks, libraries, and museums functioning as contributory to the school, as well as all other activities which provide wholesome interests for children. It makes the school, for the first time, a genuine "social center," and a genuinely "public school" in a comprehensive sense scarcely realized hitherto.[10]

In New York City

While the Gary plan was enjoying national recognition as a means to better schools, it attracted the attention of Mayor John Mitchel of New York City. Wirt contracted to spend one week a month during 1914–1915 supervising the introduction of such schools in New York where many children were attending half-day sessions. By 1918, some sixty schools, mainly in the Bronx, had been reorganized as Gary plan schools, but all had not gone smoothly. Unfortunately, since Mitchel was not a Tammany man, the Gary plan was swept into political in-fighting and became the issue in one of the "school wars" in the city.[11]

The Tammany bosses wanted to displace the Rockefeller

[10] Bourne, pp. 163–164.
[11] Diane Ravitch, *The Great School Wars* (New York: Basic Books, Inc., 1974).

interests in positions of influence in the city politics, so, through sophisticated manipulation of public opinion, they completely obscured the benefits of the Gary plan while criticizing it for failure to provide services that are beyond the scope of mass schooling. They used every ploy. Wirt was characterized as an unknown expert from a small town. His administrative arrangements were attacked as a plot of the power elite to reduce the quality of public education available to the working classes. The use of pupils in productive tasks at school was assailed as reminiscent of the Lancasterian schools—pauper schools that would place all children into a working class track, thus depriving them of opportunities, available to private school pupils, to become doctors, lawyers, clergymen, musicians, artists, orators, poets, or men of letters. Schools were depicted as having been turned into mills and factories. Shop work was interpreted as a plan to undercut apprentice programs of the unions or to produce scab labor. The longer school day was protested as interfering with pupils' after school jobs. Teachers were aroused to demand extra pay for the lengthened school day. The practice of release time for religious instruction was attacked as a Catholic plot. Gary plan school children were judged deficient, a judgment based on statistical reports of test scores which "averaged the unaverageable." It was claimed that studies were neglected in favor of exercise in the gymnasium, sitting in the auditorium, dancing, listening to phonographs, or digging in the yard. The cry was that every child had a right to a chair, and every teacher had a right to a classroom.[12] The tumult reached unmanageable proportions, not from any actual dissatisfaction with the schools, but from political interests in discrediting the mayor.

Evidently failing to understand the political forces at work, and in order to prove the worth of the plan, Wirt asked the

[12] Ravitch, pp. 195–230.

General Education Board to conduct a survey of the Gary schools. He was confident that he was accomplishing much more for pupils than was traditional schooling, and he was accomplishing it at equal if not less cost to the taxpayers. Abraham Flexner and Frank P. Bachman were assigned to conduct the survey. Flexner held positions on both the New York City school board and the Rockefeller Foundation's General Education Board, and had been fully supportive of the Gary plan innovations. However, political considerations even appear to have slanted the report of the General Education Board. Flexner's published report, for reasons only to be speculated upon, was withheld a year after the completion of the survey, and coincidentally until after the election in which the supportive mayor was deposed. A fully approving report on the Gary plan at that time would have offended the new mayor and threatened Flexner's political position.

In the attendant circumstances, the report stressed not the accomplishments, but the measure by which practice fell short of the ideals; not whether more and more varied activities were provided for a wider range of abilities and interests, but whether each of these activities was a totally controlled educational experience in terms of traditional schooling; not whether the amount of time spent on traditional subjects was equal to that in conventional school programs, but whether these activities similarly dominated the whole school day that had been extended from five hours to seven and a half.

From hindsight, details backing the complaints show the report slanted to be viewing the cup as half empty rather than half full. Assessing the activity aspects of the curriculum, the report, ignoring the social-psychological intent, questions the value of helpers in the shops and laboratories if they are not formally involved. It further observes that performance was uneven and excellence infrequent, and that the

Gary organization requires more rather than less supervision than traditional schooling. Failing to appreciate that responsibility for seeing a task through to completion is a learning experience, the report complains that pupils work at repair tasks not only until the educational need has been met, but until the job has been done. The shop instruction is faulted for stressing execution of tasks more than the intellectual aspects of the process. As a test, seventh and eighth grade boys were given written instructions for making galvanized buckets in the sheet metal shop. Although they followed the instructions efficiently and produced satisfactory buckets, their answers to questions demonstrated little understanding of the scientific principles at work in the process, or of the socioeconomic place of the steel industry in our culture. The report thus concludes that the pupils had not been led to reflect, and thus had derived little of intellectual value from their shop work [13]—by eighth grade! The cooking instruction is judged deficient because the pupils referred to recipes when preparing the school lunch instead of having memorized the proportions of ingredients. Wirt is criticized for concentrating on the administration of the whole system and leaving the direct supervision of educational activities to assistants and teachers. Certainly, in the final accounting, this is what happens in every school. Even if the instructional materials are assigned, the teacher determines how they will be used. The report questions the value to the student of the time spent helping to run the school, and it judges the physical education program to be inadequately supervised. The fact that much of the observed time in these activities was equally unorganized under traditional schooling as recess or as time not spent in school at all, is ignored. The validity of having some pupils scheduled into play activities first and study activities later in the day is questioned, when, as a matter of

13 Flexner and Bachman, p. 132.

fact, in the context of New York's half-day sessions, half of the pupils previously had not even come to school until after noon.[14] Individual study programs are characterized as poorly supervised. The example is a study of a selected seventh grade in which, reportedly, a number of children had managed to alter their class assignments without consulting anybody.[15] Certainly they consulted the teacher receiving them. The time allotted to each regular subject evidently differed from teacher to teacher,[16] as of course it does in every school.

Academic test results reported that the Gary pupils in handwriting were far above the national average for speed, but somewhat below for quality. In spelling they averaged only fifty-five per cent accuracy on the traditional word list tests, but they spelled with ninety-eight per cent accuracy in their compositions. In reading, although their oral reading skills were below average, their general reading speed and comprehension were average.[17] From these results, it could have been concluded that the Gary pupils were losing nothing academically; but the report states that "the quality of classroom instruction at Gary falls short of what is necessary." [18] Certainly this could be said about all schools. The term *necessary* has no objective limits societally. Nonetheless, these shortcomings are attributed to:

lack of unity of effort on the part of an ineffectively supervised teaching staff recruited from many sources, and to confusion due to the constant infiltration of pupils from other school systems.

In spite of the fact that this passage can be read two ways, the report sums up not that the Gary schools are accomplish-

14 Flexner and Bachman, p. 43.
15 Flexner and Bachman, p. 45.
16 Flexner and Bachman, p. 56.
17 Flexner and Bachman, pp. 90–102.
18 Flexner and Bachman, p. 102.

ing remarkably under difficult conditions, but that "Gary has not yet solved the problem of the socialization of education." [19] This was, of course, true, but it answers a question that was never asked. Wirt claimed only to be providing more and better *schooling* for the money, not an ultimate of socialized education.

In his memoirs, Flexner was moved to a self-righteous justification of the condemnatory tone of the report, mentioning among other things:

that the so-called "duplicate scheme," by which school facilities could be kept in constant use, was far from being either universal in the town or effective where it was in use; that supervision was so crude that it was impossible to speak of the system in general terms;

however, he closes the paragraph with the semi-retraction:

Nevertheless, Gary was credited with courage, liberality, and imagination; and the defects of the town could not therefore be used as an excuse for a return to the meager type of education which was fairly common in most sections of the country.

Certainly this amounts to an admission that whatever the flaws, the Gary schools were delivering services superior to most sections of the country. But he comments further:

The general effect of the report was disastrous to the exploitation of the Gary system. . . . With the publication of the report the school world was relieved, and the Gary system ceased to be an object of excitement. It disappeared from discussion as suddenly as it had arisen.[20]

Thus the report served to relieve the school world by excusing it from any serious effort to provide or administer the

[19] Flexner and Bachman, p. 105.
[20] Abraham Flexner, *I Remember* (New York: Simon and Schuster, 1940), p. 255.

extended facilities possible with the Gary plan. However, although discussion of it may have diminished, it certainly did
not disappear.

Wirt retreated to Gary and continued as Superintendent of
Schools running the work-study-play programs to the complete satisfaction of the people of Gary. By 1925, Gary had
four hundred teachers serving fifteen thousand pupils in eighteen schools. Only two of the schools were the K-12 unit
schools. The others were mainly K-8 schools. In 1927 many
of the thirty-two or so schools that had been established in
New York City under Wirt's direction were still functioning
as work-study-play schools. Angelo Patri's enthusiasm had not
waned. As principal of one of the New York schools he wrote:

I have been living with the Work-Study-Play plan for the past
ten years. I have lived faster, worked harder, lived more happily
for those ten years than in the fifteen years spent in the old-style
school. The teachers and the children have lived more enthu-
siastically, more contentedly, because of the fullness of school life.
    Varied and complete equipment—such as we have in our school,
a flexible program—such as this equipment provides, makes possible the enriched school. To me this means a truly democratic
school, a school of the people. Here each child finds opportunity
for his own peculiar talent, his own peculiar method of growth
and development. Growth fundamental to real power is made
through first-hand experiences. The day of the sit-and-listen school
has passed—thank God.[21]

There were 1,068 platoon schools to be found in 202 cities
scattered through forty-one states by 1929. By 1933 the number of these schools had doubled. However, many of them
did not incorporate the other features of the work-study-play
schools. The success of such innovative schooling ideas seems
to depend on the peculiar genius of their initiators. Wirt's

[21] Gary, Indiana, Board of Education, *The Taxpayer and the Gary Public
Schools* (Gary: Board of Education, 1934), n.p., eighth page.

death in 1938 brought an end to all promotion of the Gary plan, and the community phases of it began to disappear even from the Gary schools. A 1948 survey showed the platoon school to be on the way out, and by 1955 Gary converted to self-contained elementary school classrooms and separate secondary schools, because without Wirt's administration, the standards of achievement had not been maintained.[22]

[22] Public Administration Service, *The Public School System of Gary, Indiana* (Chicago: Publications Division of the Public Administration Service, 1955), p. 43.

4

DEMOCRATIC GROUP PROCESS
IN SCHOOLS:
CORE CURRICULUM, 1930–1955

The stock market crash of 1929 did more than just dampen the euphoria of the roaring twenties. Stop-gap economic measures failed to out-last the relief needs, and the Great Depression was settling in. Again came the questions, more pressing than ever before: What had gone wrong with our democracy? What changes were needed in the schools to turn out democratic-thinking-and-acting citizens? Enthusiasm was rallied for answering these questions, and the ensuing activity took form in school experimentation. The progressive schools of the twenties had focused on developing the creative, free child. These schools were, however, few and scattered, and were predominantly, if not exclusively, small private schools. Traditional school was certainly the norm for the nation. Nonetheless, schooling the *free child* was credited with encouraging civic irresponsibility, and the rhetoric was changed to the *whole child*, thus legitimating whatever regimentation might be deemed necessary to foster civic and political fiscal responsibility. The push was again on to turn the schools into miniature ideal democracies.

Problems of Definition

Inspired by testimonials of experimental schools organized around the cooperative group social experience, progressive educators took up their pens. John Dewey and the experimentalists had provided the philosophical orientation—that schooling for the child should be an experience of ideal democracy and should within this framework develop the knowledge and skills needed for good citizenship and personal satisfaction in living. With the publicity of the Progressive Education Association's Eight-Year Study in 1932, described in more detail later in this chapter, a tremendous number of such experimental schools became known to one another, having been started as grass roots attempts to conduct schooling in ways that could be viewed as progressive by virtue of involving the pupils in the planning. The people in charge of many of these schools had never read Dewey. They were simply taking a practical approach to the problem of stimulating pupil interest in obtaining enough education to live independent, personally rewarding lives. The literature began referring to this as *core curriculum*.

Much of the power of core curriculum to attract serious interest apparently derived from its name. Its competitors for attention—general education, unified studies, integrated studies, common learnings, correlated curriculum—all imply scattered bodies of knowledge requiring labor to bring them together into an organized whole. The name *core curriculum* is simple and it sounds like it offers a focused organization of materials, an uncomplicated unit, that teachers can easily adopt and teach to achieve whatever currently might be the popularly construed aims of education. In the hands of professors of education, core curriculum gradually lost its simplicity as a program of required conventional studies, and it became, in effect, a philosophy based on an ideal concept of the human condition with sufficient latitude of definition of terms that it could be all things to all men of good will. It apparently intended to provide guiding principles for the selection of content from all that life has to offer, but the actuality in the classroom depended entirely on the individual talent and philosophy of life of the teacher in charge. Certainly it can thus be argued that the idealized core curriculum is not a curriculum at all. Nevertheless, the effort to standardize the practices and outcomes—democracy in the classrooms to turn out democratic-thinking-and-acting citizens—continued for thirty years.

Probably the single most powerful contributor to documenting the core curriculum movement was the professional involvement of Grace Wright, a specialist in secondary education at the United States Office of Education. Initially steering clear of labels, she gathered statistics on innovative programs, conducted extensive surveys of reference materials, and analyzed data on a scale that would have been impossible to finance in any lesser agency. The published pamphlets demonstrate her most remarkable capacity to identify basic controlling factors and explain them in a simple orderly way. Four of these publications between 1950 and 1960 report the statistics she gathered. These reports also document the confusion of definitions, the variation of interpretations, the resulting incomparability of practices, and the tremendous scope of the efforts to create democratic schools.

Core curriculum had attracted Wright's attention as one of the alternatives being offered in the post-war scramble to reorganize American education in a way that would bring about a more ideal function of American democracy. In the Spring of 1949, the research and statistical service of the Office of Education sent a questionnaire to 13,816 of the 24,000 public high schools in the United States. The task of the questionnaire was to inventory offerings and enrollments in high school subjects, and Wright arranged to include one item asking for information about common learning or core-type courses. Specifically, it asked for "name of course, area of learning, or core; subject-matter areas included, if fixed; grade offered; periods per week; and enrollment." [1] She aimed to focus the definition by first researching the literature and then surveying programs for data she hoped would reveal a specific configuration of practices demonstrated to be successful in achieving the desired educational outcomes. [2]

Wright's initial question had solicited responses only on "those courses which involve the combination of two or more class periods from subjects that would ordinarily be taught separately" and which "cut across large areas of the curriculum." A second questionnaire was sent to the 545 schools reporting such a program and to other schools with core programs that had come to her attention in the interim. Her assessment in 1952 is noteworthy both for its sympathy and for its objectivity. She found mainly that the rhetoric allowed for widely varying interpretations. It reads like restatements of the common school ideal as promoted by Parker and Dewey. Some of the statements used by specific promoters of core curriculum to attract a following were:

'To provide all youth a common body of experience organized around personal and social problems'; 'to give boys and girls successful experiences in solving the problems which are real to them here and now, thus preparing them to solve future problems'; 'to give youth experiences which will lead them to become better citizens in a democracy'; 'to increase the holding power

[1] Grace S. Wright, *Core Curriculum in Public High Schools*, Bulletin 1950, No. 5 (Washington, D.C.: Federal Security Agency, U.S. Office of Education, 1950), p. 3.

[2] Grace S. Wright, *Core Curriculum Development: Problems and Practices*, Bulletin 1952, No. 5 (Washington D.C.: Federal Security Agency, U.S. Office of Education, 1952), p. 1.

of the secondary school by providing a program that has meaning for all'.[3]

Again, heavily reminiscent of Dewey, all of these are extensions of the simple fact that schools are for transmitting to youth the cultural heritage. The statements are certainly not mutually exclusive. Indeed, they can be construed as each one inclusive of all of the others.

Descriptions of programs called core curriculum had several organizational forms in common. In a core class, one teacher was assigned to teach at least two subjects in a block of time covering at least a double period. The expectation was that the traditional content could then be handled in more creative ways and thus stimulate the pupils' active interest. Exactly what a specific teacher could or would do in class to accomplish this proved impossible to regiment and impossible to stipulate in advance. Wright's concise synopsis of the spokesmen gives a clear picture of the variations in interpretation:

Most curriculum writers insist on an interpretation of core which involves a radical departure from subject-centered content and thus a departure from the study-recite method of teaching. Spears says, for example, that the core course originates from a basic citizenship objective and draws upon the subject areas replaced "for whatever they may offer in serving the general development of the students, in keeping with the goals of the course." Caswell's proposal for the core is the development of a "continuous, carefully planned series of experiences which are based on significant personal and social problems and which involve learnings of common concern to all youth." Krug recognizes as core only those block classes which have for their sole commitment "to help youth work on their major personal and social problems and needs." He specifically eliminates double-period classes which correlate, fuse, or unify subject matter and which are

[3] Wright (1952), p. v.

concerned with "the thickness of the slice rather than with the nature of the cake." To Smith, Stanley, and Shores the primary emphasis in core is on effective social living. They rule out as a major feature of core personal interests and needs of adolescents and make the assumption that a "latitude of a broad area of social living provides ample opportunity for both the play of children's interests and the satisfaction of their needs." Although these interpretations of the fundamental purpose of core vary, they all imply the complete disregard of subject boundaries and the development of problems without regard to classification according to traditional subject content.[4]

Pupils were expected to acquire skill in democratic living by actually practicing it in the classroom. Issues to be investigated by the class ideally were expected to grow out of pupils' social or civic needs and to involve: problem solving techniques, teacher-pupil planning, cooperative group planning, committee work, and activities sufficiently varied that every member of the class could contribute to the outcome while pursuing his own interests at the level of his own ability.[5] As was true with Dewey, the development of the content of the curriculum was left to the teachers. Thus the instructions could be reduced to one word, "Lead." Visits to classrooms revealed the same practices under different names, and conversely every type of classroom practice under each of the names. In an effort to get comparable returns from her 1949 questionnaire, Wright had asked respondents to designate which one of the following four types best described their program:

Type A—Each subject retains its identity in the core, that is, subjects combined in the core are correlated but not fused. For example, the teaching of American literature may be correlated with the teaching of American history. The group may be taught

[4] Wright (1952), pp. 5–6.
[5] Wright (1952), p. 6.

both subjects by one teacher or each subject by the appropriate subject teacher.

Type B—Subject lines are broken down. Subjects included in the core are fused into a unified whole around a central theme, e.g. "Our American Heritage" may be the central theme for a core unifying American history and literature, and possibly art and music.

Type C—Subjects are brought in only as needed. The core consists of a number of broad preplanned problems usually related to a central theme. Problems are based on predetermined areas of pupil needs, both immediate felt needs and needs as society sees them. For example, under the theme, Personal-Social Relations, there may be such problems as school citizenship, understanding myself, getting along with others, how to work effectively in group situations. Members of the class may or may not have a choice from among several problems; they will, however, choose activities within the problems.

Type D—Subjects are brought in only as needed as in "c" above. There are no predetermined problem areas to be studied. Pupils and teacher are free to select problems upon which they wish to work.[6]

L. Thomas Hopkins and Harold Spears had both previously listed six curriculum designs (ways of choosing content) currently being used in schools. Alberty had then presented the same six as a taxonomy of core—steps toward the most innovative program of core; core being that part of the program required of all students.[7] Wright reduced them to four, combining two of the categories in her type-B, and completely dropping the first type which was simply a list of required courses taught separately as disciplines. She reasoned that under Alberty's type-one the traditional curricu-

[6] Wright (1952), p. 101.

[7] Harold Spears, *The Emerging High School Curriculum and Its Direction* (New York: American Book Company, 1940), pp. 52–53. See also Harold B. Alberty, "Designing Programs to Meet the Common Needs of Youth," in *Adapting the Secondary School Program to the Needs of Youth*, Fifty-second Yearbook of the National Society for the Study of Education, Part I (Chicago: University of Chicago Press, 1953), pp. 119–120.

lum qualified as core, and the term became all-inclusive.
Wright even questioned the usefulness of including her own
type-A and type-B, contending that type-C and type-D were
the intended arrangements when core curriculum was
advocated.

Few if any of the reputedly successful programs accomplished any more than a loosely organized fusion of social
studies and English. Most of the descriptions give a picture
of a correlated curriculum around a cultural epochs theme
with teacher-teacher cooperation showing up as more apparent than real.

According to Wright's findings, approximately ninety per
cent of core programs replaced or included English and social studies. Only occasionally were mathematics and science
the basis for core. Evanston Township High School explained,
in part, that:

> The core class includes in its program whatever aspects of the
> environment have a bearing upon the subject matter units chosen
> for study. For instance, in the course of a week, a pupil in core
> will have had work in writing, discussions on current news, re-
> search, reporting and discussion on the chosen unit, time de-
> voted to English skills, some experience with literature or the fine
> arts and perhaps a speaker, field trip or Core business meeting.
> Core is a many-sided program adjusted to the personal needs of
> its pupils and unrestricted by departmental regulations. This ap-
> proach enables the pupil to gain a more realistic grasp of the
> interrelationships of the life about him and some perspective of
> his place in that life.[8]

Examples of a pupil activity at the Ohio State University High
School and of the subject fields to be consulted were:

> Construct and interpret a personal health record form. On the
> form, place such items as: height, weight, illnesses, accidents,

[8] Wright (1952), p. 19.

habits of good hygiene (bathing, brushing teeth, washing hair, etc.), problems of health and appearance and plans for solving the problems. Use the form to keep a health record.

Subject fields: Agriculture, Arts, Business Education, Distributive Education, Health and Physical Education, Home Economics, Language Arts, Mathematics, Music, Science, Social Studies.[9]

Whether the aim is for type-C core or type-D core, evidently the constraints placed upon the selection of a topic ultimately force standard choices. A specific activity is ordinarily formulated within one of the following ten general areas of concern: personal problems, home and family, current affairs in the world today, concerns of the school, concerns of the community, concerns of the government, democracy vs. communism, crime and punishment, conservation, and health.[10] The materials of instruction that eventually reach the hands of the pupils appear as secondary to the exercise of the process.

Core curriculum made the same demands on teachers as the Gary plan, but in a less structured way. Instead of setting up a cooperative network of specialist teachers, core curriculum characteristically gave one teacher full responsibility for integrating the program of study in English and social studies, and for drawing upon the other specialties as needed to deal with the chosen problem. In order to function adequately a core teacher would logically need to know as much or more about *all* of the discipline fields than the specialist teachers. In addition, the core teacher was expected to accomplish the traditional teaching tasks through the exercise of democratic group leadership, gaining a consensus among the pupils, guiding the formation of committees, the selection of topics, the location of reference materials, and the

[9] Wright (1952), p. 20.
[10] Wright (1952), p. 38.

traditional skills drill when a need for it was demonstrated in order for pupils to carry on the investigation or to report on it. This was an assignment for teachers constantly to create curriculum, drawing guidance from the problems or suggestions that came up in class discussions or were offered by pupils and were appropriate to the current life experiences of the particular group. It represented a tremendous extension of the Gary plan where the teacher was required only to teach the basics of a specialty and suggest application work to be taken over by other teachers specially trained and assigned to handle it.

In a program where pupils were expected to draw up a list of goals at the beginning of the year under the three headings —to improve ourselves, to improve our work, and to improve our group—one teacher had the following list of goals for herself:

1. To give students an opportunity to practice democratic living so that they may develop an understanding of democratic rights and responsibilities.

2. To help students gain skill in communications.

   a. Improve ability to write, incorporating clear thought as well as good word usage, punctuation, sentence structure, and spelling.

   b. Improve silent reading for comprehension.

   c. Improve oral reading.

   d. Improve speech through reports and discussions, with attention to clear thinking, correct word usage, and correct pronunciation.

3. To help students develop skills in identifying and solving problems pertinent to their everyday lives.

4. To develop good work and study habits.

5. To develop skills in working with others.

6. To foster an understanding of and an appreciation for the peoples and problems of the world.

7. To develop worthy ideals, attitudes, and appreciations.

8. To help students gain skill in evaluating themselves in their work.[11]

The core teacher was expected also to assume the guidance function supplanting the home room. Senior core at one school was totally a group guidance device with pupils grouped by a choice of direction: vocational orientation group, home and family life group, college preparatory group, and secretarial group. The year's work included extensive testing, discussions of the test performance with each pupil, and specific preparations for entering the next phase of their lives after leaving school.[12]

In order to accomplish these things, the core teacher presumably accepted the assignment to: exercise strong, but unobtrusive leadership; serve as a guide and leader in every phase of class activity; allow pupils to make their own decisions, but, at the same time, inject ideas of your own which will help pupils make wise decisions; allow pupils to make mistakes and then help them to evaluate their procedures and benefit from this real learning experience; allow pupils freedom to talk informally during work periods, but take preventive steps if some students interfere with the progress of others; make suggestions about the choice of projects, but not to force their choice; point out to pupils the areas in which they need work and provide situations whereby individual pupils can succeed according to their abilities.[13] In short, the core teacher was assigned responsibility for leading pupils, ages twelve to fourteen usually, in choosing, planning, and carrying out class work that would lead to mastery of the basic skills and content ordinarily included in two

[11] Wright (1952), p. 39.
[12] Wright (1952), p. 23.
[13] Wright (1952), pp. 40–41.

specific subject fields while instructing in any aspects of any other subject field into which the topic might be extended.

This presented the teacher's task as one of social engineering which required a rare combination of skills in both leadership and scholarship. Six major qualifications were outlined for the prospective core teacher:

1. Superior intellectual ability
2. Superior social and personality qualifications
3. Genuine interest in children and youth
4. Broad background of understanding of our culture in a world setting
5. Understanding of the genetic nature of the biological, psychological, and social development of children and youth
6. Understanding of and skill in the democratic process.[14]

The question of any person's ability to judge objectively whether another person possessed these traits or abilities was not addressed. The imprecision of the terms is overwhelming.

It is not surprising that few teachers elected to teach core, that teacher fatigue took a heavy toll of those who tried, and that there were so many conditions attached to the pupils' freedom of choice, the outcome was often simply school as usual.

The core program administrator was confronted with a task of social engineering more comprehensive than that of the teacher. First the personnel and facilities had to be arranged for. The problems were: procuring teachers both willing and able to constantly create curriculum; arranging for in-service teacher education in democratic class procedures; scheduling free time for specialist teachers to help, even though the demand for them was unpredictable; providing appropriate space and furniture for unpredictable projects, discussions,

[14] Harold Alberty, et al., *Preparation of Core Teachers for Secondary Schools* (Washington, D.C.: Association for Supervision and Curriculum Development, 1955), pp. 52–53.

or committee work that proved awkward in traditional class-rooms; providing much expanded library reference materials to take the place of textbooks, be the need for reading materials at seventh grade level on why the poverty problem defies solution, or how power politics operate at the national level, or how the check and balance system functions to govern what happens in economic growth and international trade; or arranging on demand whatever accessibility a group project required such as land to experiment with crop rotation, or a boat to demonstrate techniques of navigation.

Assuming that all of this was possible, the administrator was called upon to hold meetings and obtain a consensus among the various teachers working as a leaderless cooperative team, insure the approval of parents and the community, and inspire all concerned to apply themselves to the creative accomplishment of the core ideals.[15]

In reality, access to support services was severely limited in most instances, and administrators were unequal to the tasks of coordinating the program, so teachers were left to do the best they could in conventional school facilities. In addition, except for the Ohio State University High School and a very few others, the core program was limited to one or two classes or grades in a school, or was elective for a comparatively few students parallel to a regular program. The administrator thus had both types of programs to accommodate.

Given the completely flexible content of the core studies, there was little an administrator could do to establish a self-perpetuating core program. Inspiring teachers to want to run a class as a democratic group seems reasonable enough, but the core promoters never seemed to understand that all efforts at such curriculum would fail unless there was a specific, predetermined offering supported by special services and facilities. Wirt was reasonably effective in Gary, because he

15 Wright (1952), pp. 42–45.

had almost complete control. He established what would be offered in the way of facilities, instruction, and content. He made the rules. The teachers and pupils participated comfortably and confidently in a program that could have been called core curriculum and that probably came as close to accomplishing it as any later program ever did.

The Lincoln School and the OSU High School

The Lincoln School, presumably the outstanding example of ideal classroom practices, certainly had every possible support to accomplish the task. To have a new building complete with swimming pool, across the street from Teachers College, with a staff of teachers most of whom had doctorates in education, and with a three million dollar endowment from the General Education Board in 1927 to run a school for only three hundred students was true luxury. The statement of aims stresses integration of subject matter, while the orientation of the general course was to be democratic citizenship education.[16] Although the pupils were to be given the opportunity to help shape the course, the topics to be covered at each grade level were stipulated in sequence—man and his environment, early American life, living in a power age, ancient and modern cultures, and youth in America today—by then the standard topics in America's schools. L. Thomas Hopkins was there, but he did not always agree with the school's policy, at least not with what he considered to be a less than thorough way in which the aims of the integrated curriculum were carried out by the school staff.[17]

Participation in the general course was elective. The regular

---

[16] Agnes de Lima, *Democracy's High School* (New York: Teachers College, Columbia University, 1941), pp. 45–46.

[17] Personal interview with L. Thomas Hopkins, New York, 1977.

parallel offerings were: social studies, English, French, German, science (biology and physiology), mathematics, art, music, home arts, industrial arts, health and physical education. The general course, taught by a team of four of these specialists, was coordinated by one of them who remained with a group for three years—grades ten through twelve. Therefore, given the total course of study, the program must be viewed as a correlated, culture epochs curriculum rather than problem centered core. The main advantage at Lincoln School, according to one graduate, was that all of the teachers conducted their classes in a way that encouraged open discussions of the purposes, and gave the pupils a better understanding of the total program and of what they were expected to accomplish.

The same conditions existed at the Ohio State University laboratory school, which, like the Lincoln School, should have been able to produce core curriculum if such were possible. The school was started in 1932 in order to participate in the Eight-Year Study. The building was specially designed and built on the university grounds, and by 1934 housed both an elementary school and the University High School. The teachers were recruited with the specific understanding that core curriculum would predominate in the school. Many of them had doctorates, and all who did not were expected to work toward them. The teachers had the status of faculty members of the university. Although the school was supported by public funds, a small tuition was charged, and pupils whose parents wanted them in such a school came from all over Columbus. Thus, compared with other public schools, there was no community education problem, no previous program to be deposed, no tenured faculty to resist the program, no entrenched administrators, and no conventional program running parallel in the school to compete with participation in the core program. In these factors, the University High School was probably unique among the thirty schools.

The statement of aims carried the same stress on integration of subject matter, the pupil, the teacher, the school, and the community to accomplish the core objective. Their success was limited to enforcing a certain level of democratic group discussion in the core classrooms and providing excursions into the community. Although there was no published sequence of projects to be studied in the core classes, a reading of class histories reveals a specific sequence starting with a home planning unit, moving to a study of their city, and then taking up the usual topics included under national history and social problems. Student participation in planning the work in the core class was prescribed, but it was clear that specific concepts were to be taught or learned, and the skillful teacher was to direct—in the name of teaching critical thinking. The idea that curriculum actually came spontaneously from student needs is belied in a statement in the handbook for parents:

To the extent that it is feasible in terms of available facilities material, and staff, we believe that some of the school day can justifiably be spent by an individual student doing exactly what he wants to do, providing his special interest project seems worth while to the teachers with whom he is working. This does not seem unreasonable in view of the fact that he spends most of the day working on problems which a group or a teacher decides are important for him.[18]

Although the core program was required for all pupils starting in seventh grade, it was only part of the day. The total instructional program was apparently patterned after the Lin-

[18] Ohio State University School, *A Handbook for University School Parents* (Columbus: College of Education, The Ohio State University, 1954), p. 55.

coln School, with similar elective courses such that deviations from conventional schooling were more apparent than real. Similarly, the University High School accomplished only a correlated curriculum, not the integration of subject matter that was expected as an automatic result, nor the social problems democratic thinking, acting, and understanding that was written into the aims, certainly directly taken from Dewey's writing:

The statement of educational philosophy clarifies the intended integration of experience:

1. Integration of our individual, faculty philosophies of education into a growing and concerted faculty philosophy of education.

2. An attitude towards the individual student which recognizes him entire and provides for him as a unique person . . . towards "physical, mental, personal healthfulness" . . . through his "emotional and social adjustments," through the "integration of the school experience of the individual student."

3. The integration of our school community into a "generalized pattern of conduct or a way of life," the *democratic way* of living, based upon the potentially equivalent dignity and worth of the individual, and cooperation of individuals into one social group or another.

4. The integration intellectually of the individual, who sees his education as whole as life; continuously reconstructs his own philosophy in the light of experience; develops the "ability and disposition to think effectively, analytically, and dispassionately"; and "shares in the task of improving our social aims."

5. Integration of home and school (parents and teachers) as the two most important institutions carrying the responsibility of educating children.

6. Integration of school and outside communities through: study organized around functions of living; introducing an analysis of the basic conflicts just described into the curriculum; intensifying the student's opportunity to "participate, emotionally, in man's struggle to control his environment and to build himself a better civilization"; and educating toward the disposition to "share

in the task of improving our social aims." (We believe that democracy must be carried from the school community into the larger community where it is needed.).[19]

Apparently, neither the Lincoln School nor the University High School had much effect on the democratic action of their pupils out of class. A pupil at Lincoln wrote an article deploring the existence of cliques and the absence of any real feeling of cooperative group involvement, even open resistance to such efforts by some:

With such an attitude prevailing, it may be evident why class meetings end in free-for-all fights; why the Student Council is ineffectual; and why that peculiar something called "school loyalty" does not exist now.[20]

The autobiography of the class of 1938 at the University High School, in reference to group social activities, admits:

For several years the same group of students did the planning and work for these events, but practically the whole class attended them. . . .

There were many private parties given at the students' homes. As we lived in different sections of town, the problem of transportation caused the formation of definite cliques. . . .[21]

Since these two schools, with complete freedom and fully supportive administrations, failed to assemble the teacher talent and inspire the faculty coordination to bring about successful core programs, it is little wonder that experimental trial programs for only selected pupils in established, con-

[19] Ohio State University School, "Grades Seven to Twelve—Ohio State University School," *Educational Research Bulletin*, XV, No. 2 (February 12, 1936), p. 31.

[20] Joan Naumberg, editorial in *Lincoln Lore*, XV, No. 3 (April 1933), p. 12.

[21] Ohio State University High School, Class of 1938, *Were We Guinea Pigs?* (New York: H. Holt & Company, 1938), p. 223.

ventional schools had extremely limited success. They, too, could produce the appearance of core, but without the highly trained and selected teachers, the actuality was even more undistinguished. Administrators, with only token adherence to recommendations for advance planning and training, either immediately or eventually abandoned core teachers to develop the programs alone. In many schools the programs ceased after only a year or two. In some schools where there were exceptionally dedicated teachers, the programs lasted longer, but disappeared with the departure of the specific enthusiasts.

Core curriculum as outlined required constant interpersonal cooperation, constant planning sessions among teachers, and selection of new staff and teachers in accordance with specific guidelines. It evidently could not be maintained. Taking into account the settled pattern of conventional school, core curriculum universally suffered from: teacher apathy, pupil insecurity, inadequate instructional materials, unsupportive administrations, and community resistance. Always stressed was the unavailability of teachers who could or would teach core classes. More pertinent may be the fact that the core programs attempted to teach adherence to a particular value system. Values are learned in the society at large, and any attempt to conduct schooling by any other set of values is doomed to failure. Nevertheless, the history of the core curriculum movement is a story of unrelenting dedication to the ideal of a democratic school.

Hollis L. Caswell

"We couldn't find teachers who could do it." Hollis L. Caswell was talking about core curriculum while sitting comfortably on the porch of his country home in New Hampshire. "Then we were asking the impossible," was the gently of-

fered response from Arthur W. Foshay. After a pause, and in
a voice that trailed off, came Caswell's reflective admission,
"I guess we were," spoken mostly to himself as he gazed into
space. It was summer of 1978. Certainly as he lapsed into
silence, his thoughts traveled back a half century to the be-
ginning of the movement his work had inspired.[22]

It was summer of 1929 that Caswell, then age 28 and prepared with a newly acquired doctorate from Columbia Teachers College, taught his first course in curriculum at the
George Peabody College for Teachers. His experiences during
four years of teaching high school concurrent with responsibilities as principal and as superintendent of schools in Au-
burn and Syracuse, Nebraska, had impelled him to graduate
study to find out more about what he was doing. The depth
and difficulties of educational problems had become even
more apparent to him as course work in foundations of education and participation in school survey field-studies had
broadened his view and increased his appreciation of how
an educational system is organized to advance the particular
social goals and purposes of the culture that maintains it.
This had served to deepen his concern about the impact of
such a system on the lives of children as they struggled with
the school program. Believing that the task of the school was
to catch the individual pupil's interest, challenge his potential, and fit school work to his abilities, Caswell had found
no helpful organizing ideas in the courses on curriculum.
Thus, it was with some trepidation that he approached the
assignment at Peabody—to teach the summer course on curriculum. As it happened, the course attracted about thirty
school administrators and State school officials from all over
the south looking for ideas. Assured by a veteran colleague
that his *organized* ignorance was superior to their *unorga-*

[22] Personal interview with Hollis L. Caswell and Arthur Wellesley Foshay,
New Hampshire, July 26, 1978.

nized ignorance, Caswell introduced content analysis considerations that had not previously been a part of their thinking. He illustrated his beliefs with examples of the work at the Lincoln School and advocated that teachers be inspired to change the kinds of experiences children have, and to try, through their teaching, to contribute positively to the improvement of society. It was a vision of schooling as a vital influence on the lives of children, not as a routine task of memorizing and reciting.[23] His students were impressed, and opportunities for him to broaden his influence came rapidly.

Consulting first on curriculum revision in Alabama and Florida, he proceeded with dispatch, working through regional committees and soliciting the participation of teachers. In each case, within a year, new curriculum guides were produced and everyone was pleased—everyone except Caswell. The guides laid out a graded continuity geared to the development of the child. By these guides, teachers were to be able to improve their instruction. But to Caswell, instructional improvement had to be moving in a clear direction. He decided that somehow instruction in American national ideals had to be rescued from old and static formulations and be given vital content; that true democratic conduct in the real world of practical action had to be the projected outcome of schooling for youth.[24]

Virginia Guides

It was summer of 1931 that the Virginia curriculum revision program gave him the opportunity to test an all-inclusive approach. Sidney B. Hall had recently left Peabody

---

[23] Mary Louise Seguel, *The Curriculum Field: Its Formative Years* (New York: Teachers College Press, 1966), p. 142. Unless otherwise specified, details of Caswell's career are drawn from this work, pp. 137–175.

[24] Seguel, p. 147.

to become State Superintendent of Public Instruction for Virginia. He had bold ideas. He had replaced the departments of elementary and secondary education with a single division of instruction. This cleared the way for a unified approach to statewide curriculum revision, for which Caswell was called to consult. By October the Superintendent's Official Announcement proclaimed:

The development of plans for a complete State wide curriculum revision program in the elementary and high schools of the State marks a new era in the history of public education in Virginia. The fact that the public schools of the State are to have a new course of study more in keeping with modern needs is of tremendous importance, but perhaps this is not the most important aspect of the program. The widespread stimulation and growth of classroom teachers, supervisors, college administrators, and professors resulting from a serious study during the next three years of curriculum problems with all implications involved gives promise of the finest outcomes for education in Virginia.[25]

In the 1930s enthusiasm was high with the cry for the school to build a new social order so dramatically thrust on the educational community by George Counts.[26] Caswell knew that if schools were to do it, teachers had to be part of the planning and had to be both willing and able to follow the recommendations. Thus, all sixteen thousand teachers and administrators in the State were invited to take part in a study of the issues. Ten thousand accepted. Local study groups were organized and met weekly for three months. They worked from a fifteen-page syllabus prepared by Caswell. Selected readings were used as a basis for discussion of seven specific topics: 1) What is the curriculum? 2) De-

25 Dan L. Oppleman, "Development of the Revised Curriculum Program in Virginia Secondary Schools" (unpublished Ed.D. dissertation, George Peabody College for Teachers, 1955), p. 18.
26 George S. Counts, *Dare the School Build a New Social Order?* (New York: The John Day Company, 1932).

velopments which have resulted in a need for curriculum revision; 3) What is the place of subject matter in education? 4) Determining educational objectives; 5) Organizing instruction; 6) Selecting subject matter; and 7) Measuring the outcomes of instruction. Readings were balanced so that emphasis on definition and interpretation of democratic ideals was equal to emphasis on growth and development of children. Caswell realized that regardless of their willingness to learn, conventional teachers needed the security of a curriculum guide at least as a starter.

It was summer of 1932 that a group of selected teachers from Virginia were sent to the Curriculum Laboratory at Peabody, and Paul Hanna was invited from the Lincoln School to help clarify means of applying the vague criteria of subject matter, child interest, and social meaning to the choice of daily instructional materials.[27] By fall an elaborate administrative structure was operating to produce a course of study. Trial materials were circulated in 1932 and tested in 1933. Committees on social studies, language arts, science, and mathematics made up of seventy representatives from the various Virginia school districts were coordinating the work. By summer of 1934, the *Tentative Course of Study for the Core Curriculum of Virginia Secondary Schools* was finished. There is a thirty-nine-page introduction amounting to a statement of ideals. The *aims* set forth in this course outline are parallel to reasons documented by those supporting the American common school movement a century earlier:

The American system of free public schools has been developed to assist in perpetuating, improving and realizing democratic ideals. The entire school program should be projected to this end. The school should be democratic, not only in its instructional program, but also in its organization and method. . . . Consequently, the school must guide pupils in the development of types of behavior

27 Seguel, p. 153.

compatible with democratic ideals. . . . Emotionalized attitudes or general patterns of conduct must be developed which will serve as guides in meeting new situations according to the dictates of democratic concepts.[28]

Unfortunately, in spite of Caswell's expressed purpose to do otherwise, this represents only a rewording of the "old and static formulations of American national ideals." They are apparently so deeply ingrained as part of the national character that any study groups aiming for school improvement independently produce identical statements. Summarizing the several directing themes, the course of study recommends that activities, materials, and instruction provided by the school should be so varied as to: provide opportunity for successful participation by children of all abilities; increase the pupil's opportunity for greatest individual realization, which is believed to be the outcome of the development of a more democratic way of living; and provide for the pupil an educational program as broad as life itself.[29]

This unequivocally calls for a *democratic school* to turn out democratic-thinking-and-acting citizens by means of a succession of learning experiences labeled *core curriculum* by the title of the document. The provision of "vital content" was a problem and has remained so, but not for want of attention. In the course of study, the aims of education are classified under emotionalized attitudes, generalizations, and special abilities. The scope of the curriculum is manifested in a list of the *major functions of social life* to be considered under each center of interest: 1) protection and conservation, 2) production, 3) consumption, 4) communication, 5) ex-

[28] Virginia, State Board of Education, *Tentative Course of Study for the Core Curriculum of Virginia Secondary Schools, Grade VIII*, Bulletin, XVII, No. 2, August, 1934 (Richmond: Virginia State Division of Purchase and Printing, 1934), p. 1.

[29] Virginia (1934), p. 2.

ploration, 6) recreation, 7) education, 8) extension of freedom, 9) aesthetic expression, 10) religious impulses, and 11) integration of the individual. Each of these is discussed under social studies, language arts, science, and math. There are eleven *centers of interest* under which these aspects are to be considered: home and school life, community life, adaptation of life to environmental forces of nature, adaptation of life to advancing physical frontiers, effects of inventions and discoveries upon our living, effects of machine production upon our living, social provision for cooperative living, adaptation of our living through nature, social and mechanical inventions, and discoveries, agrarianism and industrialism and their effects upon our living, effects of changing culture and changing social institutions upon our living, and effects of a continuously planning social order upon our living. These can be recognized as only slight rewordings of the Dewey laboratory school sequence and of the Cardinal Principles.

The course of study goes on to detail sixty-seven emotionalized attitudes and special abilities, some of them qualified with a dozen helping statements, with the introductory paragraph admonishing in one place, "The teacher should constantly check the behavior exhibited by his pupils against this suggestive list." Two example items are:

The Attitude of Self-Integrity.
The disposition to accept responsibility for the consequences of one's acts.
Freedom from fear, worry, and the sense of inferiority.
The disposition to maintain emotional balance in the face of difficulty or defeat.
The belief in the worth of one's personality.
The tendency to face reality squarely.
The desire to be faithful to promises.
The tendency to accept criticism cheerfully.
Willingness to assume the obligations of leadership.
The urge to do all work efficiently and honestly.

The tendency to do one's full duty.

The determination to be happy.

The Attitude of Respect for Personality.

The inclination to believe in the integrity and worth of other persons.

The tendency to admire fine qualities in other people.

Willingness to let others develop their own personalities.

The disposition to insist upon fair play in all situations.

The disposition to make concessions for the maintenance of pleasant relations.

The belief in equality of opportunity.

The tendency to have consideration for the welfare and convenience of others.

The desire to cooperate with others.

The inclination to believe that personality indicates the nature of the creative force of the universe and the ultimate meaning of creation.

The disposition to regard personality as the key to the individual's success.[30]

Also included for study are 211 pages of lists of teaching suggestions, materials, and pupil activities centered on each aspect, and how to handle them in each of the areas—social studies, language arts, science, and mathematics—and they are coded to the numbered emotionalized attitudes, generalizations, and special abilities. There are, in addition, 149 pages of abilities (more recently called behavioral objectives).

Although this course of study is an extraordinarily thorough treatment of the topic, the publication is strictly aims and process oriented, giving no instructions as to the time allotted to specific items in the school day or to specific content. Exceptionally thorough study would be necessary for any teacher who tried to use this guide at all, because there are so many choices for the teacher to make in order to arrive at a course outline or plan of procedure in class.

[30] Virginia (1934), p. 3.

After the State adopted the course of study, committees of teachers spent the next six years experimenting with the reorganization of the materials of instruction to make them more readily useful for "any teacher to guide the work effectively." [31] The resulting publications, most of them carrying *tentative* somewhere in the title, cover courses of study for all grades, first through twelfth, as well as recurring statements of aims, suggested materials, and recommended evaluation procedures. It is stipulated that the core curriculum is to encompass the basic learnings required for all students and will include four years of social studies and language arts, two years of science, and one year of general math. The time allocation to the core program is to be: four periods the first year, three periods the second year, two periods the third year, and one period the fourth year. There are implications that the core could be taught by several teachers coordinated by one of them chosen to act in that capacity. The utopian quality of the expectations can be readily documented by statements from the introduction recurring in all of the guides:

In the first and second year, however, the core curriculum emphasizes experiences in more than two major fields of knowledge and if teachers are responsible for phases of the problem study involving fields in which they are not adequately trained, they should seek assistance from others who have the training necessary. A few schools have apparently achieved encouraging results by assigning all of the core curriculum work of the first year of high school to one teacher. This means that the typical situations in teaching the core curriculum for the first and second years of high school will involve a cooperative enterprise in which several teachers arrange through conferences the respective contributions in developing the problem.[32]

31 Virginia (1936), p. vi. See bibliography for full listing.
32 Virginia (1938), pp. xx–xxi. See bibliography for full listing.

SCOPE OF WORK IN THE CORE CURRICULUM

MAJOR FUNCTIONS OF SOCIAL LIFE*	GRADE I HOME AND SCHOOL LIFE (Center of Interest) Aspects of Center of Interest Selected for Emphasis	GRADE II COMMUNITY LIFE (Center of Interest) Aspects of Center of Interest Selected for Emphasis	GRADE III ADAPTATION OF LIFE TO ENVIRONMENTAL FORCES OF NATURE (Center of Interest) Aspects of Center of Interest Selected for Emphasis
Protection and Conservation of Life, Property, and Natural Resources	How do we protect and maintain life and health in our home and school?	How do we in the community protect our life, health, and property? How do animal and plant life help people in our community and how are they protected?	How do people, plants, and animals in communities with physical environment markedly different from ours protect themselves from forces of nature?
Production of Goods and Services and Distribution of the Returns of Production	How do the things we make and grow help us?	What do we do in our community to produce goods and services?	How do environmental forces of nature affect the goods produced in different communities?
Consumption of Goods and Services	How does our family provide itself with food, clothing, and shelter?	How do we use the goods and services provided in our community?	Why can communities markedly different from ours furnish us with goods we cannot produce?
Communication and Transportation of Goods and People	How do members of our family travel from place to place?	How does our community provide for transportation and communication?	How does physical environment affect transportation and communication?
Recreation	How can we have an enjoyable time at home and school?	How does our community provide for recreation?	How does the physical environment influence types of recreation?
Expression of Aesthetic Impulses	What can we do to make our home and school more beautiful and pleasant?	What do we do to make our community attractive?	How do people in communities markedly different from ours express their artistic impulses?
Expression of Religious Impulses			How do people in different communities express their religious tendencies?
Education			How do people in different communities provide education?
Extension of Freedom			
Integration of the Individual			
Exploration			

*The order in which the major social functions and the aspects of the centers of interest for each grade are presented has no particular significance.

FOR VIRGINIA PUBLIC SCHOOLS*

GRADE IV ADAPTATION OF LIFE TO ADVANCING PHYSICAL FRONTIERS (Center of Interest)	GRADE V EFFECTS OF INVENTIONS AND DISCOVERIES UPON OUR LIVING (Center of Interest)	GRADE VI EFFECTS OF MACHINE PRODUCTION UPON OUR LIVING (Center of Interest)	GRADE VII SOCIAL PROVISION FOR COOPERATIVE LIVING (Center of Interest)
Aspects of Center of Interest Selected for Emphasis	Aspects of Center of Interest Selected for Emphasis	Aspects of Center of Interest Selected for Emphasis	Aspects of Center of Interest Selected for Emphasis
How does frontier living affect the protection of life, property, and natural resources?	How do inventions and discoveries alter our ways of protecting and conserving life, property, and natural resources?	How does machine production lead to the conservation and to the waste of life, property, and natural resources?	How do social and governmental agencies protect and conserve life, property, and natural resources?
How does frontier living modify and how has it been modified by the production and distribution of goods and services?	How do inventions and discoveries affect the variety and availability of goods?	How does machine production increase the quantity and variety and change the quality of goods?	Why are governmental monopolies established for the provision of certain services?
How does frontier living restrict the consumption of goods and services?	How is the consumption of goods and services influenced by discoveries and inventions?	How does machine production of standardized goods influence the choice and use of goods?	How do social agencies influence the consumer in his choice and use of goods?
How do ways of transportation and communication serve to advance frontiers?	How do inventions and discoveries improve our means of transportation and communication?	How does machine production affect transportation and communication?	How do methods of transportation and communication affect cooperative living?
How is recreation influenced by frontier living?	How do inventions and discoveries influence recreation?	How does machine production influence recreation?	How are social and governmental organizations extending opportunities for the wise use of leisure time?
How are music, literature, and art affected by frontier living?	How do inventions and discoveries affect our art, music, and literature?	How does machine production modify art, literature, music, and architecture?	How do social organizations provide opportunities for expression of aesthetic impulses?
How is religion affected by frontier living?	How do discoveries influence the spread of religion?	How does machine production influence the development of the church?	How does the church function as a means of social control?
How is education influenced by frontier living?	How do inventions and discoveries influence education?	How does machine production influence education?	How does education function as a means of social control?

SCOPE OF WORK IN THE CORE CURRICULUM

MAJOR FUNCTIONS OF SOCIAL LIFE*	GRADE VIII ADAPTATION OF OUR LIVING THROUGH NATURE, SOCIAL AND MECHANICAL INVENTIONS, AND DISCOVERIES (Center of Interest)	GRADE IX AGRARIANISM AND INDUSTRIALISM, AND THEIR EFFECTS UPON OUR LIVING (Center of Interest)
	Aspects of Center of Interest Selected for Emphasis	Aspects of Center of Interest Selected for Emphasis
Protection and Conservation of Life, Property, and Natural Resources	How and why do nature and agencies resulting from invention and discovery affect the protection and conservation of life and property?	How and why does the change from an agrarian to an industrial order effect the use and conservation of natural resources?
Production of Goods and Services and Distribution of the Returns of Production	How does man depend upon plant life, animal life, and minerals, and how do inventions and biological discoveries increase man's use and control of nature?	How does the change from an agrarian to an industrial society affect the production and distribution of goods and services?
Consumption of Goods and Services	How do inventions and discoveries affect the well-being of the consumer?	How and why do standards of living vary in agrarian and industrialized societies?
Communication and Transportation of Goods and People	How do improved means of communication influence the behavior of individuals and groups?	How does the application of power and modern business enterprise to transportation modify our living and thinking?
Recreation	How does man adapt his play to the character of the society in which he lives?	How can recreation lend significance and beauty to the common activities of life in modern society?
Expression of Aesthetic Impulses	How do man's natural environment and his inventions provide worth while opportunities for the cultivation of aesthetic expression?	How do agrarianism and industrialism influence the development of our artistic resources and the adjustment of all individuals to their use?
Expression of Religious Impulses	How does man manifest his religious impulses through social inventions?	How do religious organizations influence living in agrarian and industrial societies?
Education	How does the home utilize social invention in the early development of 'standards of value in the child?	How does the American system of education contribute to the development of the ideals of democracy in our industrialized life?
Extension of Freedom	How and why are men denied the freedom which social and mechanical inventions make possible?	How and why does the struggle for attaining the democratic ideal modify industrialism and agrarianism?
Integration of the Individual	How can physical development and social controls promote the integration of the individual and avoid conflicts?	How can an industrialized society provide for realization of individual ideals and ambitions?
Exploration	How does man's conquest of nature aided by the spirit of adventure lead to geographic exploration and commercial expansion?	How does the spirit of pioneering influence the development of equality of opportunity both in an agrarian and in an industrial setting?

*The order in which the major social functions and the aspects of the centers of interest for each grade are presented has no particular significance.

GRADE X	GRADE XI
Effects of Changing Culture and Changing Social Institutions Upon Our Living	Effects of a Continuously Planning Social Order Upon Our Living
(Center of Interest)	(Center of Interest)
Aspects of Center of Interest Selected for Emphasis	Aspects of Center of Interest Selected for Emphasis
Why is advancement in the protection and conservation of life and property essential in a changing society and how can it be achieved?	How can nations through social planning guarantee to all the protection of life, property, and natural resources?
How can we improve production, establish an economic balance between production and consumption, and provide for a more equitable distribution of the returns of production?	How can nations plan for the establishment of proper economic interdependence by apportioning the production of goods and services and by distributing these more equitably to the consumer?
How does the advancement of science affect the thinking and the welfare of the consumer?	Used above
How do improved means of transportation and communication influence changing cultures and affect relations between nations and people?	How can modern means of transportation and communication be utilized to enhance the social welfare of nations and people?
How may changing ideas lead to the elimination of undesirable phases of commercialized recreation and promote the development of healthful and creative recreation?	How can a planning society utilize increasing leisure time to develop recreation as a creative agency for everybody?
How do culture areas and changing social institutions influence the development of the fine arts?	How can a planning society improve the quality of living for all by utilizing man's desire for beauty?
How does a changing culture affect the church as an agency of social control?	How can religion in a planning society give poise and stability to personality, motivate conduct, and foster ethical business practices?
How and why does individual and social adaptation to a changing culture make necessary constantly changing emphasis in education?	How shall social groups plan to provide for their preservation and reconstruction through education?
How do changing culture and changing social institutions make necessary a changing concept of freedom?	How can a planning society extend political, economic, intellectual, and social freedom to all people?
How can the individual maintain mental poise in a rapidly changing culture?	How can opportunity for the integration of the individual in a modern social order be provided through organized means?
How do changes in culture result from social and intellectual pioneering?	How can we plan to advance human welfare and eliminate the defects of the present social order by the spread of scientific modes of thought?

Instead of starting with the subject divisions and desired outcomes, the revised guides started by specifying a problem and dealing with its: 1) significance, 2) suggested content fields appropriate to the solution of the problem, 3) outcomes, 4) suggested ways of approaching the problem, 5) suggested leads to units of work, and 6) suggestions for developing units of work which may grow out of the leads. Phases of developing a unit of study are set out as: exploration, orientation, planning, development, and summary.[33] The topics for the first year are set out stating: the problem, its significance to society, and its significance to the pupil. In addition are given several social processes under each of: suggested content, pupil experiences, evaluation suggestions, and general references. The introduction mentions several trial scheduling plans, a suggested time allotment, and assignment of one teacher to the whole core period as desirable procedure. The guide for grade eight amounts to a study plan for a home and family unit and a safety unit. The publication for grade nine includes five such topics as illustrative problems cutting across any and all of the major social functions with leads to units of work so organized as to be assignable to the subject specialist teachers. Guides for grades ten through twelve were subsequently prepared, using *the effects of democracy on human relationships* as the area of emphasis for both grades eleven and twelve. The problems for which instructional suggestions have been made represent an awesome requirement for assembling resource materials:

First year: (1938 guide)

1. improving our provision for food and shelter and making them available to all
2. conquering disease
3. adjusting home functions and home relationships to meet the demands of modern society

[33] Virginia (1938), pp. xv–xviii.

4. meeting needs through adjusting community institutions
5. physical education
Second year: (1939 guide)
1. making the best of our natural resources
2. adjusting agricultural life to meet the conditions created by the power age
3. improving the quality of urban living
4. learning to use leisure time satisfactorily
5. physical education
Third year: (1939 guide)
1. personal relationships and adjustments of youth
2. minority racial groups
3. civic relationships
4. individual and group relations
5. the individual and his relationship to his vocation
6. buyer seller relationships
7. physical education
Fourth year: (1941 guide)
1. home and family relationships
2. employer-employee relationships
3. the relationship of propaganda and public opinion
4. international relationships
5. poverty and insecurity
6. physical education
7. safety education [34]

The teachers of Virginia acted upon all of the professional recommendations. With the full support of the state officials, surely, if core curriculum could become self-regenerating in public schools, it would have happened in Virginia. Instead, applications fell disappointingly short of expectations.

Although the excitement and the comprehensive involvement of the schools in Virginia were never to be equaled in any other state, by 1934, similar programs were under way in Arkansas, Kentucky, Georgia, Texas, and Tennessee. Alabama

[34] Taken from the tables of contents of Virginia mimeographed Materials of Instruction guides for the First, Second, Third, and Fourth years. See bibliography for full listings under Virginia.

and Florida were taking steps to continue their earlier starts. All of them were using the administrative pattern that Caswell had established, drawing on the resources of the George Peabody College. Caswell's sequence started with selected groups of teachers who would go to the summer Curriculum Laboratory session at Peabody and work out a study plan. This plan would then be published and used as a basis for organizing local groups to study the curriculum. By the end of the following summer, there would be a second guide setting out objectives for the work of the coming year for the production of curriculum materials. The coordination of all of these efforts would culminate in a guide for curriculum planning which, in effect, presented the program in a form that was expected to be followed by teachers in the schools.

Caswell worked energetically, he was organized, and he was learning. He realized that his hopes for curriculum revision in the schools could not be realized unless overworked teachers had easy access to much more information about the whole process of education with all of its social implications. So, in addition to meeting his classes at the college and consulting on state programs, he was writing his book, to be published in 1935. *Curriculum Development* was "more than a handbook, it was an attempt to structure a complete field of study, erecting a conceptual framework and fitting into it in a coherent way almost everything in curriculum making which had gone before." [35] It provided "not a polemic, but a text." [36] The section titled Social Functions Procedure states that the "curriculum should be organized so as to emphasize the major functions of group life," and that "work in all subjects should contribute to the development of an integrated program of education," and that there should be

35 Seguel, p. 162.
36 Seguel, p. 152 ftn.

"but one scope of work to which materials from all fields may contribute," and that this core should "extend throughout the school life of the child"; and he continues to describe in detail the points of view and sequential analytical steps in making curriculum choices that contribute to the recommended outcome.[37] This is the point of view he hoped would eventually take over and make it possible to have core curriculum in the high schools. Caswell writes in retrospect:

[This book] immediately achieved acceptance and for the next ten years at least was the most widely used book on the curriculum. It is in no sense oriented to the position held by the progressive education leaders of the period. It rests heavily upon experimentalism, reinterpreted and expanded by men such as those in the "Social Frontier" group. It definitely sought a balance and appropriate interaction of the three forces which I mentioned earlier as shaping the curriculum.[38]

The book includes the charts of major social functions of life from the 1934 Virginia course of study, but qualifies any recommendation of it with the observation that existing instructional materials are inadequate to carry out such a program and "many teachers, as now trained, do not have adequate background in the content subjects to deal with many aspects of the centers of interest included in an outline such as the one in the Virginia course of study, . . . [and] much greater familiarity with contemporary life is required than most teachers possess." [39] It seems Caswell viewed the Virginia course of study as a vision more than an immediate expectation.

[37] Hollis L. Caswell and Doak S. Campbell, *Curriculum Development* (New York: American Book Company, 1935), p. 174.

[38] Letter, Hollis L. Caswell to James R. Squire, January 14, 1970, National Association for Core Curriculum, files.

[39] Caswell and Campbell, p. 184.

Mississippi Guides

It was summer of 1934 that Caswell launched the Mississippi Program for the Improvement of Instruction. The process worked flawlessly, and the resulting three publications were actually edited by Caswell for focus and brevity. The *Study Program* produced that summer at Peabody was formally used by 9,315 teachers and 1,500 laymen in fifty-one groups which met for twelve sessions.[40] There was a projected five-year plan: first year, study curriculum and problems; second year, develop new materials; third year, test and teach new materials; fourth year, further revise; and fifth year, publish for general use.[41]

Under Caswell's dynamic direction, Mississippi worked through the program in three years. By the end of the second summer, there was a 228-page procedures guide setting out objectives for 1935–1936:

1. to make a beginning in instructional reorganization
2. to improve programs of work
3. to increase available instructional materials
4. to collect materials to aid in further development of the program [42]

The 1936 *Guide for Curriculum Planning* added to these objectives:

1. to accomplish an understanding of and agreement on a tentative outline of scope for the curriculum
2. to organize committees to begin production work in the various areas as outlined in the scope of the curriculum

40 Mississippi, State Department of Education, *Procedures for Production of Curriculum Materials*, Bulletin No. 2 (Jackson: State Department of Education, 1935), p. 5.

41 Mississippi, State Department of Education, *Study Program*, Bulletin No. 1 (Jackson: State Department of Education, 1934), p. 9.

42 Mississippi (1935), pp. 7–8.

3. to lay the basis for an experimental program in the reorganization of the secondary school curriculum [43]

The procedures guide stresses that all must adopt the same point of view to achieve a unity.[44] It talks about cooperative unit teaching, and gives an example of how to start with an experimental group. Since the school day has six periods, the guide suggests that teachers A, B, and C each have the group for two periods and have conventional classes for the other periods. Other specialty teachers, as *call teachers*, will help where necessary as requested by one of the three teachers who has been appointed directing teacher for the group. This is intended to be transition to what they are not yet calling core curriculum. The *call teachers* are to do work in their regular class period as directed by the directors of the activity group. When no directions are available from the activity room, " 'call teachers' will do the traditional type work." [45] The intention is integration, but this arrangement seems to take all initiative away from the subject specialist.

The Curriculum planning guide gives a chart of the division of time in the school day, and the text states:

It will be noted that it is proposed to give approximately one-half of the school day extending through the entire period of education [grades 1–12] to the phase of the program devoted to the development of social understanding and understanding of the physical environment. This is referred to as the core curriculum. It will involve subject matter from all fields and will be organized as pointed out later, around aspects of social life which are truly functional in nature.[46]

[43] Mississippi, State Department of Education, A *Guide for Curriculum Planning*, Bulletin No. 3 (Jackson: State Department of Education, 1936), pp. 11–12.

[44] Mississippi (1935), p. 16.

[45] Mississippi (1935), p. 151.

[46] Mississippi (1936), p. 45.

This program is conservative in giving a fourth of the day through grade nine to specific teaching of basic skills, reading, writing, and arithmetic. Other programs leave this time allocation to be determined by the problem chosen for the core program. Section titles under scope and sequence are repetitive of the Virginia materials and the Cardinal Principles:

1. protecting life and health
2. making a home
3. conserving and improving material conditions
4. cooperating in social and civic action
5. getting a living
6. securing an education
7. expressing religious impulses
8. expressing aesthetic impulses
9. engaging in recreation [47]

Included also are 127 listed problems grouped under these titles.[48] The criteria suggested for selection of centers of interest for a grade level are:

1. The center of interest should exert significant influence on the functional phases of life.

2. There should be numerous objects and activities within the area of the centers of interest that are of interest to children on the level for which the center of interest serves as a limitation.

3. There should be adequate instructional materials of suitable difficulty to develop the center of interest on the level for which it serves as a limitation.

4. The center of interest should provide for maximum growth of desirable concepts and should offer opportunity for participation by the pupils in significant undertakings.[49]

Using these criteria, the indicated action was undertaken:

The committee made a careful study of the characteristics of the children at various stages of development and of the major

[47] Mississippi (1936), p. 46.
[48] Mississippi (1936), pp. 61–69.
[49] Mississippi (1936), pp. 47–48.

influences on life. On the basis of this study, they defined centers of interest which they deemed desirable for the respective administrative divisions and grades of the school. The centers of interest as selected for the respective grades follow:

Lower elementary grades: life in home, school, and community

Grade 1, life in home and school

Grade 2, life in the immediate community

Grade 3, life in the extended community

Upper elementary grades: relation of life to the physical and social environment

Grade 4, life in markedly different physical environments

Grade 5, influence of discoveries and travel upon living

Grade 6, development of inventions, agencies and tools of civilization

Junior high school: the individual's adjustment to and use of the physical and social environment

Grade 7, improving the home and school

Grade 8, finding a place in the community and social life

Grade 9, using science and social and governmental agencies

Senior high school: problems and trends in living

Grade 10, problems in improving biological and material conditions through the ages

Grade 11, problems in improving social, economic, and business conditions through the ages

Grade 12, influences and trends in American life [50]

Certainly these parallel the offerings of the Dewey school.

The tone of this guide carries the expectation that all of the teachers will study it, agree with it, and do it. Laced with statements of ideals and herculean task assignments, and embracing a cultural-epoch treatment in the last three years, it is a thorough description of problem centered core curriculum. Later writings multiply specific application suggestions, but add nothing to the theory or philosophy presented in this work. Although the content is repetitious of the Virginia program, these Mississippi guides were written by Caswell.[51]

[50] Mississippi (1936), pp. 48–49.
[51] Telephone interview, Hollis L. Caswell, March 13, 1977.

The presentation is simple and carefully sequenced to be understood by non-professionals as well as professionals. Mississippi, however, did not adopt them as *mandated* for trial throughout the State. Use of them was optional. Apparently the problem of coordinating a statewide program to establish the core program in the schools loomed too large to the Mississippi State administrators, so comparatively little use was made of the guides. However, much was going on elsewhere in the nation. A government document provided the information that within the period 1928–1930, thirty-one states had formulated programs of continuous curriculum revision.[52] If Caswell's efforts in the south after 1930 are added to this number, the curriculum revision movement was already nation-wide, and the task, as viewed by Caswell and others, was to turn it to core curriculum.

It is important to notice that the activities in the south were state sponsored programs for public schools to which Caswell was directing his attention. He emphasized always that any curriculum reform, to be considered effective, must move out of laboratory schools and become the predominant method in the public schools. With the example of the Virginia program highly publicized, with Caswell's thorough treatment of every aspect of curriculum in his book, and with the perfectly organized Mississippi guides, by 1936 thorough documentation of social problem centered core curriculum was available in these publications—well before the Eight-Year Study schools had fully formulated their innovative programs. The fact that so little action could be promulgated in Mississippi should have been full warning that there were serious problems with putting it into schools, but evidently each group had to meet its own defeat.

[52] News item, *News Bulletin*, II, No. 3 (1931), p. 2. This is an early mimeographed bulletin of the Society of Curriculum Specialists which, in 1932, became the Society for Curriculum Study.

Harold B. Alberty and the Eight-Year Study

It was summer of 1937 that Caswell moved to New York to chair a new department of curriculum at Columbia Teachers College. It was that same summer that the activities at the Progressive Education Association's summer workshop focused national attention on core curriculum. While Caswell had been working in the south, another group was gathering at The Ohio State University. Inspired by Kilpatrick's *project method*, as early as 1929 Harold Alberty was voicing the concern that progressive education was focusing on individual expression and neglecting social sensitiveness which he considered equally important.[53] By 1930 he had taken up Dewey's aphorism, *education is life*, and extended it to the concept that the school could and should provide a social learning environment "as real to the child as a scientific laboratory is to a scientist." [54] By 1931 he was asking that supervisors exercise democratic leadership and "enlist the voluntary productive activity of the teachers" [55] to create a school that serves as an interpretive agency to "orient the child in his world" and assist him to "weave unity and purpose into his life." [56] In 1933, recognizing that "teachers do not universally want more responsibility," he envisions making over educational structures so "the teacher is required to assume more responsibility anyway," and he holds that using "the intelligence of the teacher . . . will result in the salvation

[53] Harold B. Alberty, "The Progressive Education Movement," *Educational Research Bulletin*, VIII (April 17, 1929), pp. 163–169.

[54] Harold B. Alberty, "An Appraisal of Dewey's Aphorism, 'Education is Life'," Abstract, National Education Association, *Department of Superintendence, Official Report* (1930), p. 152.

[55] Robert V. Bullough, Jr., "Harold B. Alberty and Boyd H. Bode: Pioneers in Curriculum Theory" (unpublished Ph.D. dissertation, The Ohio State University, 1976), p. 128.

[56] Harold B. Alberty and V. T. Thayer, *Supervision in the Secondary School* (New York: D. C. Heath & Co., 1931), p. 8.

of the school program" and "of the teacher himself." He recommends that all members of a school staff work as a team bringing about an integrated program. Supervision is promoted as a democratic enterprise to foster in the school a social spirit which "takes into account the fundamental principles of growth through democratic social living," this being the only way to avoid a regimen that is "externally imposed and autocratic." [57] This is essentially the philosophical position he retained throughout his career, and the story of his professional life can be viewed as a concerted effort to participate in any enterprises that aimed to realize these ideals in the schools.

Already intrigued by the Progressive Education Association's early organizational activities for the Eight-Year Study in 1932, headquartered at Ohio State, Alberty was destined to be instrumental in turning the innovative efforts of the participating schools toward core curriculum. The Study was backed by funding from the Carnegie Corporation of New York and the General Education Board in what were spectacular amounts for the times. Although it remains, by far, the most extensive attempt at controlled study of experimental schooling ever undertaken in the nation, it contributed much more to the education of professors about the conduct of a controlled study than it contributed to change in the form of the school experience for pupils. The plan of the Study was to free selected *progressive* high schools to experiment with alternative curriculum plans by insuring that colleges would accept their graduates. Unfortunately the planners were steeped in the *free the child* thinking that had dominated the innovative programs of the twenties. They

[57] Harold B. Alberty, "Supervision as a Means of Integrating the Total Secondary School Program," *Schoolmen's Week Proceedings*, XX (April 1933, University of Pennsylvania), p. 269.

extended it to *free the schools* and purposely left all program and policy choices to the school staffs.

Details of the purpose and plan of the Study are fully available.[58] Briefly, thirty high schools were chosen to experiment freely with innovative educational practices, and arrangements were made with two hundred colleges and universities to accept graduates from these schools solely on the recommendation of the principals. A total of 1,475 students from the thirty schools were followed through college along with one-for-one matchees in the same colleges, the matchees having attended conventional preparatory schools. Reporting on an early organizational meeting of representatives from the thirty schools held at Bennington College in 1933, Robert Leigh writes that the descriptions given were "preliminary—in some cases quite incomplete—and [represented] rather hurried activity on the part of school teaching groups." [59] Leigh characterized these plans, in the then available terminology, as predominantly the cultural-epoch organization, with a few planning to use the broad fields of knowledge organization and the organization based on the individual needs of students. Thus it was, in truth, a search for process more than a study of the effectiveness of innovative programs. Aikin wrote later, that participants should have been selected on the agreement that they would experiment with a specific philosophy and program, and that guidance should have been provided to insure some measure of comparability among the thirty schools.[60] As it was, almost $800,000 was spent promoting, recording, and measuring activities so disparate that the results had little meaning. Hindsight tells us

[58] Wilford M. Aikin, *The Story of the Eight-Year Study* (New York: Harper & Brothers, 1942).

[59] Bullough, p. 137.

[60] Wilford M. Aikin, "The Eight-Year Study: If We Were to Do It Again," *Progressive Education*, XXXI (October 1953), pp. 11–14.

that they could not have been expected to, but the search must be deemed admirable.

It was a search for ways to deal with conditions which, in the opinion of the planners, existed in the schools and should be altered. Under the heading, "Schools and Colleges Face the Facts," Aikin listed the concerns that inspired the Study and that the Progressive Education Association had hoped to remedy:

Secondary education in the United States did not have clear-cut, definite central purpose.

Schools failed to give students a sincere appreciation of their heritage as American citizens.

The high school seldom challenged the student of first-rate ability to work up to the level of his intellectual powers.

Schools neither knew their students well nor guided them wisely.

Schools failed to create conditions necessary for effective learning.

The creative energies of students were seldom released and developed.

The conventional high school curriculum was far removed from the real concerns of youth.

The traditional subjects of the curriculum had lost much of their vitality and significance.

Most high school graduates were not competent in the use of the English language.

The Commission found little evidence of unity in the work of the typical high school.

The absence of unity in the work of the secondary school was almost matched by the lack of continuity.

Complacency characterized high schools generally ten years ago.

Teachers were not well equipped for their responsibilities.

Only here and there did the Commission find principals who conceived of their work in terms of democratic leadership of the community, teachers, and students.

Principals and teachers labored earnestly, often sacrificially, but usually without any comprehensive evaluation of the results of their work.

The high school diploma meant only that the student had done whatever was necessary to accumulate the required number of units.

Finally, the relation of school and college was unsatisfactory to both institutions.[61]

As was true in the writing of John Dewey, terms abound here for which there are no objective criteria by which to judge compliance. Instructions such as "know the pupils well and guide them wisely," bring universal agreement as to the desirability of adhering to them, but the terms *well* and *wisely* have meaning only as opinions of individual human beings in specific situations. A teacher acts in accordance with his own judgment in the constraints of a specific situation as he understands it. There are no universally accepted norms. One of the chapter headings sings, "The Schools Choose the Democratic Way." Apparently the *democratic way* meant to these progressive educators that the teacher would act as advisor to pupils who, by democratic group process, would choose appropriate school experiences or projects for the class to pursue.[62] Presumably the undemocratic way is for the teacher to assign lessons for the pupils to do in the predetermined sequence of a specific discipline.

As the study progressed, there was growing insecurity in the schools regarding the unforeseen problems they were encountering with innovation. The evaluation committee was pressing for clear statements of goals as a precondition to any program of evaluation, and the schools could not produce them. Freedom was not enough. The schools began asking

[61] Aikin (1942), pp. 4–11.
[62] Aikin (1942), p. 25.

for direction. By 1936, the requests for help were coming in such quantities that the staff could not meet them. The staff needed a way of determining what or whether a centralized system for helping could be established, whether there were common needs, whether types of helps or direction could be standardized or categorized, or whether the helps, indeed, had to be tailored to each specific situation, and if so, how such help could be provided on a large scale.

It was summer of 1936 that *workshops* emerged as the means to providing the needed help. The idea seems to have evolved from Caswell's curriculum laboratory summer sessions for teachers. Starting with a group of thirty teachers invited to attend a six-week session at The Ohio State University to work with the problems brought by the teachers, by 1939 the workshops sponsored by the Progressive Education Association were too numerous to tally, and school systems all around the nation were sponsoring such gatherings. Alberty had been heavily involved in these workshops. Their function was inspirational, and Alberty's concept of core curriculum had become the sought-after program for secondary schools to so inspire the pupils; however, inspiration is one thing—the capacity to command the forces to put it into effect proved to be an entirely different matter.[63]

It was summer of 1937 at Sarah Lawrence College that the delegation of teachers from Des Moines discarded the *basic aspects of living categories*, advocated by Alberty in *Science in General Education*, having found that these determinants were so non-specific that they had not been helpful to teachers of Des Moines. The group adopted instead, a modified list of categories from the Mississippi curriculum guides that had been written by Caswell. The differences were of seman-

[63] Angela E. Fraley, "Core Curriculum: An Epic in the History of Educational Reform" (unpublished Ed.D. dissertation, Teachers College, Columbia University, 1977), pp. 43–44.

tics only, not of substance. The difficulty was apparently in finding prescriptions sufficiently precise to direct the choice of instructional materials. It was summer of 1938 in Denver that Alberty's group from Ohio State produced a set of guidelines that became the accepted criteria for selection of core activities:

They recommended that the core program include only those units, activities, or problem areas which:

1. are common to large groups of pupils, if not to all;
2. are persistent or recurring in human experience, or are related to, or are illustrative of, such problems;
3. are not likely to be handled well by any of the traditional subjects;
4. require, or would profit from, cooperative planning, teaching, and learning;
5. call for exploration in several areas of experience (as health in biology, recreation, the home, sex, care of children, public health, health hazards in industry, the consumer, safety, etc.);
6. require orientation in a wide range of relationships and implications for their significance to become apparent (for example, the corporation—as related to mass production, advertising, absentee ownership, labor problems, propaganda, war, imperialism, pressure groups, etc.);
7. require consideration of various points of view in addition to factual data (as race relations);
8. require larger blocks of time than conventional periods (as, community study and participation);
9. call for relatively continuous experience rather than a unit course (for example, the arts are not strictly "problems" but kinds of experience which should be included in the core curriculum);
10. extend the application of such objectives as techniques of thinking, work habits, study skills, social sensitivity, creativeness, etc., over a wider range of experience than the traditional subjects;
11. require a minimum of specialized laboratory equipment;
12. do not require extended drill in specific skills (as, taking three months off for drill in typing or percentage or cabinet making);

13. do not require sudden extension or drastic modifications of present levels or work habits and study skills (as, a sudden shift from lesson learning to complete responsibility).[64]

In addition, this group listed suggestions for core activities using as categories the four *basic relationships of living* from *Science in General Education*—personal living, immediate personal-social relationships, social-civic relationships, economic relationships. Choices were listed under each category. Under personal living, for example, was the first division, personal health (physical and mental), and suggestions were: heredity, native endowments, habits, learning, intelligence, normal variability, eugenics, diet, drugs, developing personality traits, etc. Thus, they added something, but not enough. The groping continued for some specific directions that would make it possible for "any teacher to guide the work effectively." The same problem that confronted Virginia in 1934 was still unsolved—teachers could not do it.

Accordingly, much time at the workshops was spent developing resource units on the social areas to be covered in the core program activities, but these were found not to be generally useful for specific application. The usefulness of this activity, of benefit only to the participants, turned out to be the experience of *applying* the underlying principles— a practice that could be carried over into daily planning.[65] However, the need for the security of having something in hand such as a resource unit was clearly shown by the types of questions and projects the teachers brought with them to the workshops.[66] The Tulsa group was quite direct about it:

We don't know any scientific way of arriving at grade placement of materials or units of work, but we can never put a new program

[64] Quoted in H. H. Giles, S. P. McCutchen, and A. N. Zechiel, *Exploring the Curriculum* (New York: Harper & Brothers, 1942), p. 50.

[65] Giles, p. 75.

[66] Giles, p. 82.

into effect unless our teachers know ahead of time what they are expected to teach.[67]

Although each group studied and came to their own conclusions, the conclusions seem stereotyped, because they had, in effect, been predetermined by the reference materials available for study, and, indeed, by aims of education believed to be compatible with the ideals of the nation's founding fathers.

The heavily funded evaluation committee of the Eight-Year Study under the direction of Ralph Tyler did strikingly innovative work in developing tests and scales for measuring social attitudes in an attempt to assess the social learnings presumably newly being taught by the recommended core curriculum. The Study continued until 1940. The reported conclusions were at best, nondirective. After ten years and an expenditure of $800,000, they could state only that the students from the experimental schools performed as well academically in college as their matchees from conventional schools, and that students from the more experimental of the thirty schools slightly out-performed their matchees in participation in student activities. The over all conclusion was that there is no one best way to prepare students for college. The Study, unfortunately, failed of rigor in the initial planning in two ways. First, in a way that seems completely unreal from hindsight, freedom was simply given to the schools to innovate in any way they wished. Overlooked was the fact that freedoms are not always exercised. Second, the practices to be evaluated were neither defined nor controlled. A reading of the case histories of the thirty schools reveals that the deviation from standard practices in the majority of the schools existed mainly in the written statements of aims. Actual innovative practices defied statistical comparison, not

[67] Giles, pp. 98–99.

only among schools, but among classrooms within the same school, and traditional lessons occupied much of the time in most of the schools.

The five volumes that reported the Eight-Year Study in 1942 remain a monument to the field of curriculum at that time. The first volume presents the Study, giving a description of the intent and a review of events. The second volume describes in detail the curriculum philosophy, development, activities, problems, and conclusions. The third volume gives a detailed account of the work of the evaluation committee, the requests for help, the tests devised for measuring social attitudes, and the many variables left unattended. The fourth volume describes the detailed follow-up activities at the colleges and universities, the problems encountered, and the conclusions. The fifth volume contains separate reports from all of the thirty schools describing their experiences with the innovative programs.

Unfortunately, this report was published coincident with the entry of the United States into World War II. The democratic form of government in Europe was falling before the totalitarian war machines. The immediate demand on the United States was to meet might with might and to prevail, at least to stop the totalitarian takeover of western Europe and thus to insure that there would not be a concentration of strength sufficient to attack the United States. Educational innovation was set aside. Tried and true methods were used for technical training to prepare for entry into national defense industries or the military service.

It will never be known how much the war crisis was responsible for the disappearance of the programs that were part of the Eight-Year Study. Certainly if they had the potential of continuing at all they should have been well enough established after eight years to endure a period of diverted attention. It is known that by 1950, when Frederick Redefer went back to the schools to look, most of the innovative programs were gone, and those that remained had lost their excitement and power. He found mostly conventional school as usual. Not only had the attempts at integration of subject matter and pupil participation in planning been dropped, but in at least one case the desks were again screwed to the floor in traditional rows. Many of the programs were assessed as not having been strikingly innovative ever.[68]

There were sporadic follow-up studies over the next twenty years, each one adding to the accumulating evidence that the activities of the search had no lasting impact. It is true, the conclusion of the study had documented that students from the thirty schools did as well in college academically as their matchees, and were somewhat more active in student affairs. It did not document any marked superiority that would justify the added expense and energy required to conduct the innovative programs.[69] Twenty years later, a follow-up showed that although students from the thirty schools still expressed belief in the democratic philosophy, their civic activity was no different from the norm of their socio-economic level.[70] This indication of failure to act in accordance with the social attitudes as measured by the tests seems to justify the conclusion that pupils were reciting the correct answers rather than expressing the convictions or beliefs that governed their own behavior. But the idea of a democratic school, it seems, has an intrinsic appeal to American educators and is ever renewable.

In a mass publicity effort by the United States Office of Education from 1945 to 1952 to bring about nation-wide

[68] Frederick L. Redefer, "The Eight-Year Study—Eight Years Later" (unpublished Ed.D. dissertation, Teachers College Columbia University, 1952).

[69] Redefer (1952).

[70] Margaret Willis, *The Guinea Pigs After Twenty Years*: A Follow-Up Study of the Class of 1938 of the University School, Ohio State University (Columbus: State University Press, 1961).

democratic conduct of schooling, *life adjustment education* emerged as a short-lived umbrella term which was in essence another name for core curriculum:

Life adjustment education is designed to equip all American youth to live democratically with satisfaction to themselves and profit to society as home members, workers, and citizens. It is concerned especially with a sizable proportion of youth of high school age (both in school and out) whose objectives are less well served by our schools than the objectives of preparation for either a skilled occupation or higher education.[71]

At a work conference two years later, listed as next steps were: community improvement, interdisciplinary research, coordinated programs and services, improvement of professional personnel, curriculum planning by total community, evaluation by demonstrated competence (not Carnegie units), work on changing college entrance requirements, and experimentation with changes.[72] These certainly were the standard innovative objectives found in the educational literature since Dewey started writing about education.

Another publication was purportedly "to suggest means by which members of a school faculty can work together in developing their educational program to better meet the life needs of their pupils . . ." It goes on to say that the list of guiding principles is selective rather than exhaustive; however, item 4 for example, reads globally:

4. *Emphasis is Upon Direct Experience:* In life adjustment education programs the common personal, political, social, and economic problems of individuals along with those of the local community, State, region, and Nation are made the basis of special concern and study. The emphasis is upon direct pupil-teacher planning, sharing, and participation in real-life experiences while

[71] Federal Security Agency, *Vitalizing Secondary Education*, Bulletin 1951, No. 3 (Washington, D.C.: Office of Education, 1951), p. 36.
[72] *Vitalizing Secondary Education*, p. 45 and pp. 103–104.

seeking solutions to individual, social, and civic problems. Such an approach requires the abandonment of the concept of "extra-curricular activities" and makes excursions, travel, community surveys, school-work programs, study, and hobby clubs and any other form of direct experience for pupils integral parts of the educational program.[73]

Thus, the focus was identical with core curriculum, the Gary plan, and the Dewey and Parker schools.[74]

The extent of the activities of the commission leaves no doubt that every high school in the nation knew about the life adjustment education movement, but there is little evidence that anything effective was done about it at the classroom level. In the opinion of one researcher, it was simply a "sprawling curricular prescription, subject to as many interpretations as it had interpreters . . . [and] functioned as a slogan, not a discrete curriculum program." [75] The commission's *guiding principles* to set the attitudes that would govern a program in a school were, in brief:

1. respects individual worth and personality . . .
2. enrolls and retains all youth . . .
3. requires courses and course content concerned with problems of living . . .
4. emphasis is upon direct experience . . .
5. planning, organization, operation, and administration are democratic . . .
6. records and data are used constructively . . .
7. evaluation is for desirable changes in pupil behavior . . .[76]

[73] Federal Security Agency, *Developing Life Adjustment Education in a Local School*, Circular 1949, No. 253 (Washington, D.C.: Office of Education, 1949), p. 5.
[74] as discussed earlier in this book.
[75] Dorothy E. Broder, "Life Adjustment Education: An Historical Study of a Program of the United States Office of Education, 1945–1954" (unpublished Ed.D. dissertation, Teachers College, Columbia University, 1976), p. 69.
[76] Broder, p. 71.

Although the parallel of these statements with statements by the core curriculum enthusiasts is absolute, remarkably, life adjustment education and core curriculum are treated as separate entities in the literature. This, in spite of the fact that the same individuals were writing about both programs and the same programs that were called core curriculum were cited as examples of life adjustment education. The attendant literature had picked up also the ten "imperative educational needs of youth" that had been stated so boldly by the Educational Policies Commission in 1944:

1. All youth need to develop salable skills and those understandings and attitudes that make the worker an intelligent and productive participant in economic life. To this end, most youth need supervised work experience as well as education in the skills and knowledge of their occupations.

2. All youth need to develop and maintain good health and physical fitness.

3. All youth need to understand the rights and duties of the citizen of a democratic society, and to be diligent and competent in the performance of their obligations as members of the community and citizens of the state and nation.

4. All youth need to understand the significance of the family for the individual and society and the conditions conducive to successful family life.

5. All youth need to know how to purchase and use goods and services intelligently, understanding both the values received by the consumer and the economic consequences of their acts.

6. All youth need to understand the methods of science, the influence of science on human life, and the main scientific facts concerning the nature of the world and of man.

7. All youth need opportunities to develop their capacities to appreciate beauty in literature, art, music, and nature.

8. All youth need to be able to use their leisure time well and to budget it wisely, balancing activities that yield satisfactions to the individual with those that are socially useful.

9. All youth need to develop respect for other persons, to grow

in their insight into ethical values and principles, and to be able to live and work cooperatively with others.

10. All youth need to grow in their ability to think rationally, to express their thoughts clearly, and to read and listen with understanding.[77]

These can be tallied almost one for one with the *major functions of social life* in the Virginia materials for core curriculum of 1934, which in turn are little more than elaborations of the Cardinal Principles of Secondary Education of 1918.[78] Certainly there is, functioning here, an underlying universal, which may well be the human being.

These innovative educational efforts were more than just ideas that never took shape. When the programs came under attack, proofs of effectiveness were widely sought. The indicators of effectiveness that lent themselves to documentation were: status studies to show incidence of core programs—how many schools had them, when they had started them, plans to extend them to more grades, plans to start new programs; follow-up studies; opinions of pupils, teachers, school administrators, professional educators, teacher trainees, and parents all expressing enthusiasm for core; and descriptions of successful programs in action. A fairly accurate tally of these factors resulted from Wright's surveys. She concluded that core curriculum in 1952 was not commonly found in America's public secondary schools. An estimated 833 of the nation's approximately 24,000 secondary schools, or 3.5 per cent, had adopted it. Most of these programs were concentrated in cities in seven states—California, Maryland, Michi-

[77] Educational Policies Commission, *Education for All American Youth* (Washington, D.C.: National Education Association, 1944), pp. 225–226.

[78] Commission on the Reorganization of Secondary Education of the National Education Association, *Cardinal Principles of Secondary Education* (Washington, D.C.: Department of the Interior, Bureau of Education, Bulletin, 1918, No. 35).

gan, Minnesota, Missouri, New York, and Pennsylvania. They were mainly in the junior high school grades and were English and social studies combinations.[79] By 1957, incidence had increased from 9.7 per cent to 19.3 per cent,[80] and in 1960 to approximately 25 per cent, a combined figure for both junior high schools and junior-senior high schools.[81]

These figures, however, require some interpretation. In the light of Alberty's warning in 1951 that "it is unsafe to draw any conclusions when a school reports a core program," [82] because of imprecision of definition and interpretation, Wright's problem was understandably much more than just counting programs as one would count school buildings or pupils enrolled. Although the percentages are small, the numbers are large enough to have tested the feasibility of the recommendations. One can estimate the figures to mean that as many as 2,000 schools were experimenting with block-time scheduling, freeing teachers to use core curriculum methods in 1960. However, in the years from 1930 to 1960, many such programs were tried and discontinued. In addition, the count was not weighted to reflect the size of the core program reported. A school was included in the count whether it had one experimental class involving one teacher and twenty pupils, or included the whole school involving twenty teachers and a thousand pupils. Thus, attempts to conduct democratic schools under the several names included thousands of

[79] Wright (1950), p. 28.

[80] Grace S. Wright, *Block-Time Classes and the Core Program in the Junior High School*, Office of Education Bulletin 1958, No. 6 (Washington, D.C.: Department of Health, Education, and Welfare, 1958), p. 1.

[81] Grace S. Wright and Edith S. Greer, *The Junior High School: A Survey of Grades 7–8–9 in Junior High Schools and Junior-Senior High Schools, 1959–1960*, Office of Education Bulletin 1963, No. 32 (Washington, D.C.: U.S. Government Printing Office, 1963), figures extrapolated from p. 20.

[82] Harold B. Alberty, "The Core Program in the High School," A recording (Educational Recording Services, 6430 Sherbourne Drive, Los Angeles, California 90056), lecture recorded in December of 1951.

teachers and tens of thousands of pupils all told. Many of the programs were heavily documented down to the smallest detail of classroom conduct, and transcripts of discussions and planning sessions were made available for emulation. Wright compiled detailed bibliographies with hundreds of entries, but no methods emerged that could be meaningfully communicated and replicated independently of individual teacher talent. The recurring difficulties with core curriculum remained: inadequate classroom space, failure of acceptance by the remaining traditional elements in the school, unsupportive administrators, unavailability of reference materials, lack of reliable evaluators of social learnings, resistance of parents, and finally the unavailability of teachers capable of handling core classes, which was and still is probably of more significance than all of the others put together.

Questioned about core curriculum in 1977, Caswell wrote:

The most distressing thing about the whole effort to develop a core concept and practice to implement it is that so little if *anything* remains of the effort. This is true I fear of most efforts to develop new practices in education. The same problems persist today in substantial degree as were present in 1930–40. Yet one can predict with some degree of assurance that innovations of today will suffer the same fate as those of yesterday, —which raises the question of how educational development can build on the experience of yesterday to achieve gradually but certainly improvement.[83]

It is said that if we fail to learn history, we are forced to relive it. Apparently innovative schooling projects consistently relive the errors of the past over and over again.

[83] Letter, Hollis L. Caswell to Angela E. Fraley, March 13, 1977.

5

SCHOOLS TO PRESERVE
A DEMOCRATIC WAY OF LIFE:
FORD FOUNDATION PROGRAMS,
1950–1970

Fund for the Advancement of Education 1951 to 1961

The implications of the programs sponsored by the Fund for the Advancement of Education must be assessed from a double perspective. First, through the aims of the Fund, and second, through the activities of the programs in the schools. In the aftermath of World War II, in response to the outcry for strengthening our democratic institutions, the Ford Foundation fashioned a policy statement listing program areas for the advancement of human welfare: 1) the establishment of peace, 2) the strengthening of democracy, 3) the strengthening of the economy, 4) education in a democratic society, and 5) individual behavior and human relations. To the traditional rhetoric of the democratic ideal, the report adds an unusual insight into the meaning of democracy as a way of life:

The democratic way is dedicated to the freedom and dignity of the individual as an end in himself.
The antithesis of democracy is authoritarian, wherein freedom

and justice do not exist, and human rights and truth are wholly subordinated to the state.

The democratic course is the choice of the peoples in free countries of the world, and perhaps the hope of tens of millions who are now citizens of totalitarian states. But the making of the choice is not a single, simple act of selection; it is a way of total living, and to choose it means to choose it again and again, today and tomorrow and continuously and forever to reaffirm it in every act of life.[1]

Paralleling the language of Joseph Mayer Rice fifty years earlier, the report judges the nation's educational system to be in a sorry state:

In considering the functions of formal education, the Committee recognized that democratic objectives require three things of our educational system: first, that it apply in action the principle of equality of opportunity; second, that it train citizens and leaders in coping with society's problems; and third, that it assist all men to employ their native capacities not only to make a living but to carry on satisfying and purposeful lives. In all three respects our educational system is thought to exhibit serious deficiencies. . . .

Our educational system faces numerous other problems, such as the great shortage and often poor quality of teaching personnel at the primary and secondary levels; the pressure of enrollment upon physical plant during the growth of the postwar school population; the apathy of parents and other citizen groups toward school requirements; the difficulties of obtaining adequate financing, particularly in regions of low economic potential; and the slowness with which schools adopt new procedures and aids for teaching. . . .

Perhaps the greatest single shortcoming of our school system is its tendency to concern itself almost exclusively with the dissemination of information. Schools should be the most important influence outside of the home for the molding of whole persons. The function of the school is the broad training of mind and intel-

[1] Ford Foundation, Report of the *Study for the Ford Foundation on Policy and Program* (Detroit: The Ford Foundation, 1949), p. 47.

lect. Yet individual purpose, character, and values, the bases of which are laid in the home, are often inadequately developed by the institutions which could, by precept and deeper teaching, assume a major share in supporting them most successfully. To concentrate on the absorption of information seems unrealistic when one realizes that students retain only a small portion of such information. Education must meet the needs of the human spirit. . . .[2]

How to solve these problems in the interest of society as a whole, and how to do so without at the same time undermining freedom of education itself, constitutes a problem of a still higher order in the application of democratic principles.[3]

Acting on the premise that:

A foundation may enter controversial areas boldly and with courage as long as it maintains a nonpartisan and nonpolitical attitude and aids only those persons and agencies motivated by unselfish concern for the public good,[4]

the Foundation addressed this "higher order" problem of educational change by establishing the Fund for the Advancement of Education in 1951. Evidently on the basis of insufficient historical research, the problems were viewed as previously unattended. According to the Fund's assessment of schools:

Quality suffered, furthermore, from the very extension of secondary education. The American people encouraged this spread of an ideal without stopping to formulate the purpose of secondary education, or systematically attacking the problems inherent in simultaneously educating the bright and the dull, the scholarly and the worldly, the artistic and the Philistine, the native-born and

[2] quoted in Ford Foundation, A Foundation Goes to School: The Ford Foundation Comprehensive School Improvement Program 1960–1970 (New York: Ford Foundation, 1972), p. 7.

[3] quoted in Ford (1972), p. 8.

[4] Ford (1949), p. 67.

the immigrant. In consequence, by midcentury the typical high school was a hodgepodge of disparate persons and programs, and its curriculum was a potpourri of college preparation, vocational training, and adjustment-to-life. It had been thrown together in the effort to satisfy everyone; not surprisingly, it satisfied very few.[5]

To set its activities apart from those funded by a flood of government money allocated to education, the Fund expected selectively:

to encourage new thinking, underwrite experiments and demonstrations, and support pilot programs that were too uncertain of success or too controversial to be paid for by public tax money or private endowment funds.[6]

Free of public pressure, it assumed it could "assist and stimulate existing institutions to test many a promising avenue of change." [7]

It was for these same purposes that the Progressive Education Association had structured the Eight-Year Study in 1931. If the Fund read the resulting publications, it failed to heed the message—clear in the report of 1942, and directly set forth in a 1953 article [8]—that specific experimental practices must be agreed upon by all participants, that detailed advance planning of innovations must be done, that careful controls must be exercised if the programs are to be evaluated in any meaningful way, and that the evaluation mechanisms must be built into the original plan. Instead, the Fund apparently used the same type of program selection the Eight-Year Study used, failing even to include plans to coordinate projects. They were inspired by:

[5] Ford Foundation, *Decade of Experiment: The Fund for the Advancement of Education 1951–1961* (New York: Ford Foundation, 1961), p. 13.
[6] Ford (1961), p. 15.
[7] Ford (1961), p. 15.
[8] Aikin (1953).

the increasing willingness of schools and colleges to engage in fruitful experimentation, and by the strong evidence that under the direction of imaginative and energetic educators certain lines of experimentation contribute constructively to the advancement of education,[9]

and evidently the Fund selected programs on the basis of such expressed willingness. The selections were explorations into: fifth year programs to prepare college graduates for teaching who had not elected it as undergraduates; teacher aides; fellowships for advanced study; team teaching; use of audio visual aids, T.V., tape, and teaching machines for better staff utilization; training of minority teachers; education for exceptional children; bridging the gap between school and college; up-dating course content; establishing experimental colleges; and bringing modern business methods into school financing—all geared to find ways of delivering quality education with fewer teachers.

In the interest of freeing these "imaginative and energetic educators," approximately five hundred grants totaling fifty million dollars were awarded. Apart from the few topical specifications above, the money was given almost *carte blanche*. The recipients could choose what they would produce with it. The Fund, accepting project directors' reports rather than asking for formal experimental plans and data, at the end of ten years had little to show. The absence of a master plan requiring programs to test specific innovations in specific ways precluded any comparative analysis of successes or failures. The difficulties were honest ones. Project directors' jobs proved to be stepping stones to bigger and better things, so directors changed frequently, and their replacements had different ideas, kept changing plans, and time was lost.

In the distribution of funds among the several areas of interest, the "recruitment and training of teachers" received

[9] Ford (1961), p. 9.

about twenty-five million dollars (half of the total). The other twenty-five million was allocated mainly to "better use of teachers' time and talent." Programs for "extension to all of full educational opportunity commensurate with ability," "improvements in curriculum," and "improvements in school management and finance" received comparatively token attention.[10] Thus, efforts to deal with the course content in creative ways were limited. New math, science, and social studies materials were researched. To the extent that one thinks of varied scheduling, the use of audio visual aids or programmed instruction as curriculum, these things were encouraged, but mainly as devices to maintain an accepted standard of instruction with the proportionally fewer teachers available.

The conclusion of the 1951–1961 period of experimental programs were:

1. A number of projects reveal new ways to ease the teacher shortage and raise the quality of instruction—by drawing on unused human resources and building new incentives into the profession.[11]

2. A variety of new technqiues, using both human and mechanical aids, can make the top-notch teacher available to far more students in the course of the working day and the school year.[12]

3. To further the ideal of equal opportunity for all to be educated to the limits of their abilities, these programs have sought to overcome the handicaps of geography, poverty, and race.[13]

4. The gifted and the average student, and all of society, as this series of projects indicates, will benefit by radically overhauled courses, more flexible time schedules, and collaboration between the high schools and the colleges.[14]

5. The academic world has ignored the modernization of busi-

[10] Ford (1961), p. 19.
[11] Ford (1961), p. 25.
[12] Ford (1961), p. 43.
[13] Ford (1961), p. 69.
[14] Ford (1961), p. 81.

ness methods and financing, but several studies show how newer methods can raise both the quantity and quality of education.[15]

Questions posed for the Fund's continued attention in the ensuing decade reflect a recurring pattern of educational theorists' to talk in terms of societal universals and to imply that the problems are a reflection of inadequate schools:

The past decade has been deeply concerned with a series of critical problems in education. All of them pertain to the central issue of how schools and colleges can maintain or improve quality in the face of exploding student enrollments. Some notable gains have been made, but as we enter the Sixties, a number of urgent questions remain unanswered.

Can the function of the schools be clarified? Only to the extent that we are clear about the goals of education can we devise satisfying school and college programs. And it is plain that we can determine educational goals only after we have answered the larger question of what it is that we as a nation value most and wish above all else to accomplish in the years ahead.

Can the curriculum be designed anew to reflect all we know and still have to find out about the learning process? Schools and colleges must provide common learning that is broad and rigorous and at the same time they must meet the specialized demands of a complex society.

Will the teacher shortage be solved? Will we have to depend on traditional approaches or will we find new and better ways of utilizing teaching talent? Can we raise the status and economic level of the teaching profession and thereby attract a larger number of able people?

Will it be possible to develop schools that challenge and capture the interests of youth in the depressed neighborhoods of large cities?

Can we work out a better basis of financial support for our schools so that children in Mississippi will have the same educational opportunities as children in New York or California?

Building on the experience gained in the Fifties, will we find

[15] Ford (1961), p. 95.

ways to bring all sound new ideas and techniques together to achieve not just a patchwork of improvement, but a coherent design of advancement? Such a unified effort would include curriculum reform, expansion of the team-teaching concept, provision for flexibility of student grouping as well as of time schedules, and the imaginative use of modern means of communication in the classroom; it would mean a more and more effective partnership between school systems and institutions of higher learning in the training of teachers and in educational research and development.

And above all else, can we improve our educational programs to make the most of human talent? In the pursuit of excellence we cannot afford to sacrifice the variety our educational establishment must maintain if it is to provide equality of opportunity to all.

New ideas and experiments will be needed in the decade ahead. For education is a creative process in which "principles that have served their day expire and new principles are born."

The Fund for the Advancement of Education is proud to continue to play its part in meeting one of the most serious challenges that face our nation in this revolutionary age.[16]

Since consensus does not exist on societal goals or on what level of compliance constitutes adherence to them, it is unreal to assume that any more uniformity can be gained in schools than exists in the society at large. "What we as a nation want most" certainly is relevant to consideration of, for instance, a compulsory education law, but a school deals with individuals, not the nation. Nevertheless, the educational program of the Ford Foundation spent the next decade trying to find out what we as a nation ought to want in our schools.

The Comprehensive School Improvement Program, 1961 to 1970

In 1961, the Fund was replaced with the Comprehensive School Improvement Program (CSIP) charged with the task of:

[16] Ford (1961), pp. 104–105.

bringing together a sufficient number of the new practices to create a *critical mass*—a chain reaction of change that would overcome the inertia of school systems and produce significantly different educational institutions. The new program was to provide a capstone for the projects of the past decade, consolidating gains and encouraging large-scale implementation.[17]

For every phase of activity, there were numbered criteria:

It sought to encourage simultaneously the following practices: 1) team teaching, 2) the use of non-professional personnel in schools, 3) flexible scheduling, 4) variable size pupil groups for instruction and new space arrangements, 5) the use of audio-visual resources, including educational television, 6) programmed instruction, 7) language laboratories, 8) educational data processing by machine, 9) independent study, 10) advanced placement and early admissions, 11) nongraded school programs, and 12) school and university partnerships for curriculum improvement, and pre- and in-service teacher preparation.

Underlying these specific practices were four key assumptions that helped shape the programs: 1) that the purpose of a school is to promote learning, not teaching; 2) that learning is a continuous process and must be related to an individual student's abilities and needs; 3) that curriculum in all content areas should be built on a continuum from the beginning to the completion of formal education, rather than be frozen by grade levels or age of pupil; and 4) that there needs to be a constant and continuous examination of the ways by which schools facilitate learning in order to take advantage of discoveries and developments.[18]

The only items above that were not specifically included in the Gary plan of 1908 are educational television and machine processing of data. And there is a further parallel to what Wirt achieved in Gary and what CSIP only hoped for:

An additional ingredient necessary for the critical mass was the involvement of as large a unit of the educational system as possi-

17 Ford (1972), p. 9.
18 Ford (1972), p. 9.

ble—ideally all staff members at all grade levels and in all content areas of a particular school.[19]

Thus the belief was that ideal circumstances could be provided in which to demonstrate the desirability and possibility of including all twelve of the recommended practices in the same school. The successes of these programs scattered about the nation were expected to inspire neighboring schools to adopt a similar conglomerate of practices and effect nationwide school improvement. There were three criteria for selection of projects: 1) local objectives were in harmony with the objectives of CSIP, 2) staff sophistication was sufficient to handle the necessary array of innovations; and 3) the financial resources were sufficient to continue the programs, if desirable, once Foundation funds were no longer available.[20]

The Newton Public Schools

Innovative programs of the Newton, Massachusetts, public schools received almost a million dollars of the Ford Foundation funds distributed by CSIP. Newton qualified for these funds by virtue of a long history of school reform programs, some of them in collaboration with Harvard professors of education. Their philosophical outlook was certainly in keeping with the trends of the period, and their innovative efforts had provided patterns that were adopted by other school systems. Newton serves here as an example, because the programs were varied and thorough, and publications documented activities throughout the funded period, thus making readily available the information needed for comparisons to earlier educational change efforts. In addition, of the thirty existing programs in 1959, four of them already had Ford money either directly or indirectly.

[19] Ford (1972), p. 9.
[20] Ford (1972), p. 9.

Planning conferences started in 1959 geared to use CSIP money in Newton. The original idea was to concentrate all of the grant to create one fully integrated exemplary K-12 unit in compliance with the CSIP purposes. This plan had to be modified for political reasons. It was believed that the inevitable comparisons among the *haves* and the *have nots* would disrupt the whole school system and defeat the innovative program. Thus, although Newton carried on approximately 120 programs between 1959 and 1969, they varied in duration from three-day workshops to curriculum change programs continuing through eight years. They varied in scope from production of a science manual to total school reorganization for continuous learning. There were several sources of funding, only one of which was CSIP. Fifty-four of these programs (45 %) were partially funded with Ford money.

A few of the longer range projects were selected for detailed description in the eight-part report. The Hamilton (elementary) School and Meadowbrook Junior High School programs are reviewed here. Although each of these was viewed as a different approach to school revision, the differences were only in the starting points. For instance, individualized instruction, continuous learning (non-graded) organization, and team teaching in some form occur as an inseparable configuration. One does not occur without the others implicit.

The Hamilton School in Newton became a non-graded, or in terms more to their liking, a continuous learning school. Planning started in 1959 under the impetus of an enterprising and talented principal. Initial steps took place in 1962 to make the change. The listed objectives were:

1. To eliminate the artificial barriers erected by "promotion" and "passing" or, "not passing" procedures,—such standards to be met by a certain date in June.
2. To be more realistic about our knowledge of children and how they grow.

3. To set for the slower child a more appropriate pace in which to learn the basics of arithmetic and reading particularly without needless repetition in these and other areas.

4. To eliminate the practice of holding back a bright child by keeping him on grade level in reading and arithmetic, although we claim to meet his needs by so-called enrichment.

5. To eliminate some of the repetition of teacher preparation, i.e. (1) three teachers preparing lesson plans for children in grades 1, 2, 3, reading on second level; (2) three teachers working on individual activities for individual or small group instruction in all four major subject areas.

6. To lessen labeling children as stupid or bright by non-promotion or double-promotion. Because of the multiplicity of materials available in this kind of grouping, labels would be more difficult to attach than [in] a self-contained classroom.

7. Finally, to meet the needs of the individual better than in self-contained classrooms.[21]

By 1968 the objectives were extended on the premise that the school could influence or alter community values:

We therefore seek to find a way of extending the "humanistic" goals of the Hamilton School into the community—whereby we would try to create opportunities for pupils, teachers, parents and others to work toward:

1. Development of human potential and self-regulation for all.

2. Acceptance of a wide variation in personality, style, and behavior as legitimate and desirable.

3. Greater flexibility intellectually, socially, emotionally, and therefore less rigidity in dealing with one another and with ideas.

4. Greater knowledge of appropriate behaviors . . . and possible alternatives in making decisions and acting on choices.

5. Greater skill in communication among and between pupils, parents, teachers and other members of the community.

6. Greater skill and new ways of working cooperatively.

7. Understanding and skill in dealing with each other correc-

[21] Lillian Ambrosino, "The Hamilton School Experience," in *Blowing on a Candle: The Flavor of Change*, ed. by David Whiting (Newton, Massachusetts: Newton Public Schools, [1972]), Appendix 1-A, p. 1.

tively rather than punitively when failure to live up to appropriate behavior occurs.[22]

Priorities for our school in terms of our *instructional* program are very ordinary. Among top priorities are the teaching of skills in reading, writing, speaking, listening and computation. In guiding ways of creative and disciplined thinking including methods of inquiry and application of knowledge; to encourage competence in self-instruction and independent learning; to guide pupils to a fundamental understanding of the humanities and the arts, mathematics, the social sciences, natural sciences and to begin to develop an appreciation of and discriminating taste in literature, music and visual arts, and to provide instruction and services in health and physical education.[23]

Certainly these are simple restatements of Parker and Dewey and core curriculum. In a residential district of relatively uninvolved employed parents, Hamilton had only 200 pupils and a staff of eight professionals. Political and economic extremes were not part of the conditions. The principal wanted non-grading not as an experiment to see what might happen, but as a change in structure necessary to the controlled individualized instruction she viewed as desirable. An elaborate scheme for grouping and scheduling pupils had to replace formal grades. Some form of cooperative teaching had to replace the self-contained all-subject classroom. A planned intermingling of children of different ages to promote social understandings required considerations of academic ability and temperament.

Scheduling was reminiscent of the Gary plan. Group A had language arts while Group B had mathematics for the first half of the morning, and they traded places for the second half of the morning. Eventually, these two studies were spread over the whole day with smaller groups. There was a kindergarten, a primary unit for ages six to nine, and an in-

[22] Ambrosino, App. 1-D, p. 3.
[23] Ambrosino, App. 1-B, p. 2.

termediate unit for ages eight to eleven. The half-day kindergarten had a teacher and a student teacher. The primary unit had a unit leader (one of the teachers), curriculum area specialist teachers, a part-time (Harvard intern) teacher, a teacher aide 10 hours a week, and student teachers. The intermediate unit had a similar staff. Planning became sufficiently complex that school opened a half-hour later on Fridays to give extra time for teams to meet and plan the following week. Summer workshops contributed to the feeling of working together.

In 1965, the principal moved on to reorganize another larger school and was replaced by a principal who judged that Hamilton was pre-occupied with structure and organization and was neglecting "human matters." She worked toward a more relaxed and open atmosphere in which these "human matters" that she considered to be the motive for wanting non-grading could be stressed. Her plan in 1966 focused on pupil self-concept:

1. The concept of man and the concept of self as a free agent operating in a field of change must become the basic working tool of all learners.

2. The assumption that the acquisition of knowledge and cognitive skills can be divorced from the processes of healthy personality development and self-understanding is no longer tenable. Therefore the school must be seen as a socializing agency that can provide experiences and conditions likely to encourage behavioral freedom, one where knowledge of self and environment and feelings towards self are recognized as being co-extensive.

3. This assumes a new role for the school psychologist. No longer would he be considered an expert or provider (or giver) of tests and results. Now, he would become almost a partner in the process of education, especially in training teachers to develop self-concept.[24]

---

[24] Ambrosino, text, pp. 18–19.

Thus, inspired by Bruner's 1960 rediscovery of discovery learning, the principal's philosophy took on the language of the *whole child* approach of 1918. The school's responsibility for the individual child's progress was understood to include the physical, social, psychological (or emotional) and the academic:

The learning process was "conceived as a uniquely individual function through which human beings organize, integrate and extend their experiences on the basis of past experiences. . . . It becomes the synthesis of subjective and objective meaning. Teaching (then) is a facilitation of experiences to encourage the synthesis and free expression of objective and subjective meaning. . . . Maslow's horticultural model of Bruner's self-discovery were seen as most consistent with maximizing opportunities for learners to actively discover the meaning for themselves and to employ individual choice on the basis of this meaning." (1966 *Proposed Plan.*) [25]

After three and a half years, this principal moved on, and a third principal entered the program:

To this principal, the concept of non-gradedness is an agreement among teachers to be open-minded and open-ended. It embodies both a philosophy and a structure. The first promotes ". . . a way of working with youngsters, by helping them to be curious, to question and discover. . . ." The organization, on the other hand, encourages the teachers to overlap in subjects, age levels and in their own relationships with other teachers. Both are necessary, in her opinion, for the problem posed by this system is the communication of success and failure to children—an extremely sensitive and intricate process; . . .[26]

She interprets freedom as having limits, clearly defined and consistently applied. Traffic in the halls was a problem, so the schedule was reorganized to minimize it. . . .[27]

[25] Ambrosino, text, p. 19.
[26] Ambrosino, text, p. 24.
[27] Ambrosino, text, p. 25.

Acknowledging the accomplishments of the preceding period of sensitization, she now feels the time has come to return to the child's academic side. She writes in her first report, dated March, 1969: ". . . The records on children are not complete. We understand their behavior quite well, but little is known diagnostically. We need to set up our own skill sheets on each area in each level, or we need to adopt somebody else's ideas on what a child should cover at each step. We need to know what they know."

She hopes to develop with the teachers a "flexibly concrete" instrument that will define and sequence skills, especially for reading and math. Such a diagnosis will supplement her staff's "knowledge, intuition and judgment," and help them to begin teaching with a definite awareness of what should be covered. This is her priority.[28]

Certainly these are the first steps to a return to *school as usual*, albeit with a more complicated scheduling plan. The school was on its third principal, and only two of the original staff of teachers remained.

The usual curriculum subjects were scheduled: reading, language arts, spelling, listening activities, writing, mathematics, science, social studies, music, art, physical education. Initially all teachers were to teach all subjects, planning the instructional materials with the team, but making their own worksheets. This proved impossibly time consuming with the multi-age grouping. Changing to departmentalized instruction reduced the number of subjects for a teacher, but increased the number of pupils to plan for. It was discovered also, that apparently the teacher in a self-contained elementary classroom teaches reading not only at the formally planned time, but throughout the day in connection with instruction in all of the other subjects. At Hamilton it became necessary to assign all teachers responsibility for some reading instruction in order to maintain acceptable pupil achieve-

---

[28] Ambrosino, text, p. 25.

ment. This, it will be recalled, was a requirement in the Gary schools and in Parker's school.

Continuous learning added many responsibilities for the teachers at Hamilton. The heaviest of these was the creation of curriculum materials for individual progress. Teachers had neither the time nor the expertise to do it. Since the program attracted a great deal of attention and many visitors, there was a felt pressure to "make it work smoothly," when, indeed, the necessary flexibility precluded a smooth operation. Team leaders were eventually dispensed with, and the teachers (only three or four to a team) simply met and conferred among themselves.

The spontaneous integration of subject matter possible in the elementary self-contained classroom required advance planning in the non-graded team-teaching school, therefore very little integration took place. Group cooperative learning activities seldom occurred owing to the difficulties of coordinating individual schedules to assemble appropriate groups. It will be recalled that the Gary plan had solved this problem with auditorium, shop, and gymnasium periods in a lengthened school day.

Although Hamilton was heralded as a successful continuous learning school, and the average achievement test scores of the pupils were maintained, any gains in the social, emotional, or self-concept aspects of pupil growth remain unmeasured. A highly talented principal set it up. Exceptionally dedicated teachers and heavy funding kept it going. When the same principal organized Horace Mann School as a continuous learning school (with twice the enrollment and staff) it took an entirely different form. Pupils were assigned to specific units ranging from a self-contained one-teacher classroom to team-taught flexibly scheduled groups, with pupil assignment depending on somebody's periodic evaluation of individual social, emotional, and academic needs. Apparently, Hamilton as a pattern was not transferrable.

When Meadowbrook Junior High School moved into continuous learning, the various aspects of organization had different significance. There were approximately 980 pupils and 36 teachers. In 1962, a "randomly selected" group of 161 pupils and six teachers became a pilot project.[29] By 1966, there were 500 pupils in the non-graded units. At this time, the decision to eliminate the traditional program offerings and place all pupils in continuous learning units touched off a controversy that became nationally known.

Initially, at Meadowbrook the concept of non-grading was not to be viewed simply as an organizational difference, but as a whole different view of the learner. The philosophical ideals, assumptions, and premises guiding the program were listed in 1962. The philosophical ideals were briefly stated:

> That inherent in man's existence is the right to develop his individual potential.
>
> That given the opportunity, man will select goals which are beneficial to both self and society.

Assumptions related to the learning process were listed:

> That learning is evidenced by a change in perception and behavior, and that the most meaningful learning takes place through the process of inquiry and discovery for oneself.
>
> That relationships are uniquely drawn from an experience by each individual.
>
> That there are similarities among individuals and differences among individuals.
>
> That learning can best take place when the individual has freedom of choice.

[29] Alison Evans, "The Meadowbrook Experience," in *Blowing on a Candle: The Flavor of Change,* ed. by David Whiting (Newton, Massachusetts: Newton Public Schools, [1973]), p. 1.

That the individual reacts to a stimulus, initiates action and progresses at a rate and depth which may be independent from other members of a group.

That learning takes place best when an individual makes a personal commitment to and becomes involved in his own education and its selective use.

Premises upon which the project was built were listed with respect to knowledge, the child, the teacher, the environment, and the school:

That knowledge is that ever growing and changing body of information which man has collected about himself and his world. Involved in this body of knowledge are his techniques of gathering, classifying and using this information.

That knowledge can be useful in and of itself, and can be used for building attitudes and developing patterns of thinking.

That there is no prescribed amount of knowledge which all children must hold in common, although there may be certain minimal standards toward which each individual should work.

That the child is in the continual process of individual growth and learns in a transactional process between his own goals and the goals set by society.

That there is a direct relationship between meaningful learning and the amount of personal, dynamic involvement.

That the child has rights and responsibilities as an individual and as a member of groups.

That the teacher has the primary task of contributing to a change in the perception and behavior of the student.

That by providing opportunities for freedom of choice, the teacher helps the student accept the responsibility for his own education.

That in fulfilling this task, the relationship between the teacher and pupil should be viewed as a transactional one where the teacher acts as a resource person.

That learning situations must be provided at many levels, in different groupings, and enhanced by a variety of approaches to meet the varying individual needs.

That the environment must be one which provides for integration of experiences, offering a daily opportunity to meet in a situation which encourages a feeling of belonging and security.

That the student must have the chance to think and work as an individual and as a member of a small group composed of various age levels in a situation which is free from the pressures of subject content.

That a daily opportunity must also be provided for learning to take place through the process of inquiry and discovery by a personal commitment to a task.

That the school should be considered an institution which is specifically designed to provide a setting within which the child may prepare for the place he will make for himself in society.

Grouping for guidance took a somewhat complicated form:

The 161 pupils in the Alpha Unit were separated, at random, into 12 houses. Each house contains pupils of varying ages, experience, and social and academic development. The houses have been assigned to six House Advisors, each of whom is responsible for two houses containing approximately 14 children. The houses meet with their advisors daily either in the morning between 8:00 and 9:00 or in the afternoon between 2:00 and 3:00. These house meetings are designed to provide opportunities for:

Advisors to meet with individuals, small groups, or the total house group.

A pupil and advisor to meet to discuss individual progress in specific subject areas (see contract progress charts).

Pupils to make their weekly plans.

Pupils to make their daily plans.

Pupils to work on their contracts.

Pupils to help one another.

Pupils to plan for group activities, such as inter-house scholastic and athletic competition, social affairs, art festivals, school publications and assemblies.

Pupils to plan or hold school government meetings and programs. House meetings are free of any specific subject-matter content. House pupils and advisors can use these meetings as they see fit.[30]

[30] Evans, text, pp. 4–7.

With the exception of the contract arrangement, this certainly describes core curriculum shuffled among several teachers instead of just one. Excerpts from an article by Jonathan Kozol echo the core curriculum testimonials:

The kids are neat and scrubbed and lively. They are 11, 12, 13, 14, 15. They walk along gleaming corridors, arms loaded with books, eyes bright, mouths moving, elbows shoving. They talk about Thoreau, about Katherine Anne Porter, about Vietnam. They talk about Macbeth and about The Paris Review and about Bobby Dylan and Janis Ian and Joan Baez; they talk about Tito's brand of Communism and about the reasons behind the Spanish Civil War. . . .

They are pupils in the seventh, eighth and ninth grades at Meadowbrook—showplace of the educational system of Newton, Mass., itself one of the few really great school systems of the nation. And they are among the few children left anywhere in public education for whom the claims of life, breath and free air have not been subordinated to the demands of someone else's ambition. . . .

Students, for example, really do select the courses that they wish to study. This does not mean simply the kind of choice that is offered between French and Latin or between English I and English II. It involves a variety of choices as to content, difficulty and instructor which rivals the choice given to students in many of the country's largest universities, and far exceeds the choice available in many of the smaller colleges. . . .

"In a school like Meadowbrook you can't hide failure," the Principal says. "We have one faculty meeting a week, sometimes two. When things go wrong, we sit there and discuss it. I've got to emphasize that we are not fooling when we talk about pupils making choices. They do choose and, if they don't choose *us*, then we're the ones who have to worry."

The high emphasis on choice brings out a great deal that is not generally perceptible in much of public education. The failure of a teacher to be chosen is one obvious index. Another, though less frequent, is the failure of an occasional pupil to make any choice at all, or his inability to justify the choices he is making.

In most schools a pupil who lacks energy or feels drained of initiative will still go through the rituals of obedience, showing up for classes, propping himself in the back row and often managing to hold up a textbook somewhere in the vicinity of his nose. He may suffer his way through the course and stumble his way through school.

The difference at Meadowbrook is that a pupil who feels that way will sooner or later probably stop making it to class. Since no one tells you where to go, you've got to decide it on your own. When a pupil starts wandering the corridors, teachers recognize right away that he's in trouble. Apathy is highly visible.

The frequency, as well as the fact, of choice is important. Classes do not run year-long or even term-long, but generally for eight weeks. At the end of every eight-week period, a pupil is asked to look hard once again at where he is heading and where he has been and to decide if he is likely to arrive by this course at the place he really wants to go. . . .

The School makes use of expensive I.B.M. equipment to keep a close watch on every child. Pupils each day are requested to make a "learning center" selection for the day following. By choosing a card programmed for a center, the pupil automatically enters his name on three lists. One goes to the director of the center, so the center will know how many pupils to expect. Another goes to the pupil's "House Advisor," a teacher who is responsible for watching over the patterns of choice that his pupils make and who meets with them daily in groups of 12 for a half-hour. A third list goes to a central office for the school's use in research, in keeping records and in keeping track of what each child is doing.

The I.B.M. procedure which has tended traditionally to depersonalize institutions of all kinds, is employed at Meadowbrook to grant pupils far more personal independence than they have ever had before. In a very specific sense, children are both more free and yet more scrupulously watched, more independent and yet more intimately aided and advised than would seem possible within almost any other public junior high.

What happens at Meadowbrook if a teacher or House Advisor believes that a pupil may be growing too highly esoteric in his choice of courses or in his choice of learning center? What does the advisor do, for example, if he feels a child may be damaging his future by failing to choose the kind of preparation he will need to get to college? "In such a case," according to the Principal, "the House Advisor will try to point the pupil toward the problem by appropriate questions rather than by steering. We feel that the process of choosing is every bit as important in the long run as the rightness or wrongness of the choice and we do not really want our pupils to take orders from a House Advisor."

When an advisor, or a teacher, sees a situation where he would like to express his own strong personal opinion, he is expected to be certain that the pupil is exposed at the same time, or shortly thereafter, to an opposing view. Meadowbrook is not interested in manipulating pupils to conform to adult values, and teachers do not believe that getting pupils onto the right road for college is inherently valuable unless it has something to do with the personal convictions and inner direction of the child.

Sometimes, visitors to Meadowbrook don't know quite how to react. A staff member recalls a school administrator . . . who came in to look at a colonial history class: "The teacher was in shirt sleeves listening to a noisy argument about something—I don't remember what. Four girls were off by themselves in another corner, talking softly. One boy, a little devil, was trying to get a map of the 13 colonies into the center of the screen but he couldn't seem to do it. Finally he went over and tapped another boy on the shoulder. They fiddled with the projector for a while and at last they got it working. The little one looked so happy.

"Meanwhile, the main group was still arguing. The teacher was just leaning on his elbows and sometimes trying to get in his own ideas if he could. The [visitor] was flabbergasted. . . ."

The children and teachers at Meadowbrook like . . . it best when not only the pupils, but the teachers, too, get into the act and argue with each other. . . .

Last year, more than 200 educators from almost every state and several foreign nations came to take a look at Meadowbrook and many more will soon be coming.

"We always try to caution them about one point," says a staff member. "Don't take the gimmicks without the philosophy behind them. This school is not just a package of innovations—it's a whole way of thinking about children. It's easy enough to imitate nongrading, give up marks, introduce discussion classes and use contemporary novels. It's another thing to really believe that children are o.k., that they start out good, that they start out sensible, that they can really teach one another, that they've got things to teach their teachers. It's one thing to say that you're taking your teachers off their pedestals. It's another thing to actually do it and not have the plaster crack apart." [31]

This, of course, was the view of a sympathetic, perceptive, and highly articulate school reformer who saw mainly that the stresses of external discipline had been removed, and that the pupils felt free. It implies that much was gained and nothing of value was lost. Teachers presumably recognized and attended to pupils who did not choose college preparation, pupils who chose at random, or pupils who wandered the halls, failing to choose at all. Teachers were expected to solve these problems by indirect questioning rather than by direct recommendations to pupils. It can be argued that this is a distinction that does not make a difference. In the one instance the pupil is told what is expected, and in the other instance the pupil is left to guess what is expected. In both instances the only pupil choice is to do it or not to do it.

Whether all of this freedom still accomplished the purposes of school was brought into question by some negative opinions of some worried parents:

The kids there are just out to pasture. It's a waste of time.

It functions under the shroud of intellectual dishonesty. It is irrelevant to the life of the child.

Meadowbrook is a farce. . . . It promises individual help for kids but it doesn't deliver. . . . I had to have my older girl tutored to make up for what she lost in class.

Meadowbrook doesn't give children the fundamentals they need in English and math. . . . It's unfair that parents don't have a

[31] Jonathan Kozol, "A Junior High That's Like a College," *New York Times Magazine* (October 29, 1967), p. 32.

choice and that youngsters have to stay in Meadowbrook while the city's other junior high school pupils are getting the bread and butter of education—the real essentials.

Until colleges stop testing and relying on competitive grades for admission, it is ridiculous for a junior high school to operate as an ungraded program.

You're just behind the 8-ball if you can't afford a private tutor. (A particular cause of bitterness from parents was the fact that many mothers were forced to go back to work to get the money to pay private tutors. . . . Inordinate numbers of college-bound students in this affluent community accrue credit to the Newton school system with the aid of outside, supplemental instruction.)

Many Newton youngsters are sacrificial lambs to Continuous Learning—it operates with more concern for the experiment than for the child.

In addition to parents, there were teachers at Meadowbrook who had their doubts:

We're pretty sure that statistical evaluation wasn't valid . . . although we think some parts of CL are constructive, we worry privately about what we're doing to the lives of these kids particularly when we see the chaos in the Learning Centers where they're supposed to use their free time to advantage every day.

The League of Women Voters got into the discussion and conducted a survey. The usual criticisms were voiced. Multi-age grouping imposed academic limitations on the older pupils in a class. Frequent grade reports are evidently a substantial motivator to many pupils, and this was lost with the practice of only one grade assigned at the end of the year. There were no minimum demands made of pupils who were either too immature to choose for themselves, or who were not *self-motivated*. The study centers were chaotic, over-populated, inadequately directed and ineffective. Teachers were too overloaded to give the necessary attention to each pupil, and there was insufficient formal instruction in the basic subjects.[32] So traditional offerings gradually replaced the innovations, and Meadowbrook returned to being a very good junior high school.[33]

Problems and Criticisms

In view of all that had been done and written since 1900, the failures of the Ford programs could have been predicted at the outset. Caswell in 1936 had listed all of the details that needed to be attended to. *The Story of the Eight-Year Study* in 1942 had documented the pitfalls of failure to attend to these details. The core curriculum literature carries account after account of problems that proved insurmountable. Yet the *lessons learned* section of the Ford programs report reads like a summary of the literature since the turn of the century:

Before 1965 . . . the Foundation and much of the nation still held the attitudes of the 1950s: innovation was regarded as stylish and even as an end in itself rather than as a means to a more crucial overhaul. The schools and the Foundation displayed little urgency about whether the undertaking actually addressed the root problems facing American education, and even less concern about whether the projects related to the larger underlying social and political problems of the nation.[34]

By the mid 1960s, consideration of the larger impact was required: ideas needed to be shared; conflicts arose as the community became involved or aware; planning and coordination were necessary to equalize opportunity, and:

an "evaluation revolution" had begun, raising profound questions about the outcome of all of these projects. It was becoming ob-

[32] Evans, text, pp. 29–32.
[33] Evans, text, p. 47.
[34] Ford (1972), p. 26.

vious that simply funding projects would no longer be enough and that better ways would have to be developed to monitor their impact as well.[35]

Errors during the formative period of CSIP proved to be the program's undoing:

Project objectives were stated in such a vague and global manner that it was impossible to say with any certainty whether or not they had been reached. Goals were often stated in *input* or *process* terms, on the assumption that changes, *per se*, would produce better education. Relatively little emphasis was placed on the actual educational *outcome* of the projects.[36]

Evidently it took the Coleman Report of 1966 to explode the myth that spending more money meant better education or more effective schooling.[37]

The objectives of staff utilization programs were mostly unrealized by CSIP:

In summary, while substantial amounts of Foundation and federal monies were being allocated to teacher-preparation programs at the college level, CSIP directed more attention to specific school situations. Because the majority of CSIP teachers continue to function in self-contained classrooms, it is impossible to assess the permanence and depth of changes generated by innovative projects; i.e., changes in teacher behavior and in classroom style, or modification of teacher attitudes toward students and toward curriculum. The most subtle and significant changes in these areas do not depend on formally restructured classrooms. On the other hand, the use of paraprofessionals—a trend that the Foundation helped reinforce—has clearly resulted in permanent change, introducing new cadres of people into education, providing channels of

[35] Ford (1972), p. 26.
[36] Ford (1972), p. 12.
[37] James S. Coleman, *et al.*, *Equality of Educational Opportunity* (Washington, D.C.: Department of Health, Education and Welfare, Office of Education, 1966).

access into schools for many more blacks and for those without previous formal training, and encouraging many nonprofessionals to fulfill formal requirements for certification.[38]

The production of instructional materials by teachers was unrewarding:

But despite the packaged curriculum movements, widespread commitment to develop curriculum within each project required a heavy investment of teacher time. Under the rationale of local uniqueness, project teachers almost universally felt the need to create their own materials. There is no overall assessment of how much of this material was generated. It also is not known precisely whether teachers were simply unaware of recent curriculum units that were readily available or whether they were conditioned to resist the so-called "teacher proof" units regardless of their quality and availability.

In many instances, the overproduction of inadequate curriculum units at the local level was not the fault of the individual projects. Rather, the projects were doing what they had been funded to do. The Foundation staff itself had underestimated the difficulties in producing new curriculum units. . . .

In terms of both cost and student teacher learning, the adoption of professionally developed curricula produced far more substantive change than in-house curriculum development.[39]

The adaptation of technological equipment apparently required skills uncommon in teaching staffs:

The overall contributions made by CSIP in the use of technology were limited. . . . In far too many instances, . . . equipment of all kinds is gathering dust. The on-going costs of maintenance and production are much greater than originally anticipated and have been accentuated by the financial crisis now facing schools. In general, the use of such equipment has fallen off markedly within the projects. . . .

[38] Ford (1972), pp. 19–20.
[39] Ford (1972), p. 21.

A wide variety of hardware was available, but software was scarce and of poor quality.[40]

Apparently flexible scheduling and grouping plans produced an insurmountable problem of monitoring students' free time. It meant that the whole operation had to be coordinated throughout the total staff of the school.[41] Innovations in staff utilization were least fraught with problems, because they did not attract community attention. New curriculum materials were successful only at the whim of individual teachers:

Modular scheduling and independent study, for example, create an atmosphere that challenges the notions of order, discipline, and learning traditionally associated with schools. As students of any age are given more freedom to talk, to move, and to decide where, when, how, and what to study, parents, community, and even teachers become apprehensive that the culture is being eroded.[42]

Almost as a disclaimer, and directly parallel to the conclusions of the Eight-Year Study, the report states:

Above all, however, the CSIP experience demonstrated that physical facilities do not necessarily dictate the type of instructional program. Very creative programs did occur in the most traditional settings, and very conventional programs could be found in modern facilities.[43]

In addition, as was true with the Eight-Year Study, the training and visibility which accrued from participating in the programs sent the leaders to bigger and better positions within the existing system instead of teaching them how to improve it or change it.

[40] Ford (1972), p. 22.
[41] Ford (1972), p. 23.
[42] Ford (1972), p. 25.
[43] Ford (1972), p. 24.

PART II

THE REALITY:

THE ART OF THE POSSIBLE

6

DEMOCRACY AND SCHOOLING: CONFUSED LABELS

Dewey's philosophical treatises on democracy and *education* provided incentive, but not guidelines, for applying democratic principles to *schooling*. Nobody can argue with the premise that schooling in a democratic society somehow must prepare citizens to function in a democratic society. Logic thus dictates that such schooling be conducted in accordance with democratic principles so that pupils will experience democratic group process in a cooperative community. The idea of a cooperative community implies not only the choice and consent of the governed, but the participation of each person as both governor and governed. This means that all ability levels are viewed as contributing something of value. There is equal opportunity and freedom for every individual to develop initiative and to have his individuality and his opinion respected by the group. In addition, each individual works cooperatively with the group, and is responsible for exercising individuality only to the extent that it functions in accordance with the good of the many. Instances of conflict are to be settled by discussion and consensus, and all share alike in the common good. Under these directives the task of the school becomes the task of demonstrating that making value choices based on the good of the many serves self-interest better than other possible choices. Efforts to conduct schooling on these principles can be successful only to the extent that each individual chooses these standards of personal conduct, and acts in accordance with them.

The movement for democracy in the classroom was an attempt on the part of professional educators to include the teacher as a person and the pupils as persons in the stated offering of the school—to define and structure the experience of human interaction in such a way that the good life would be the predictable outcome. Specifically, the outcome was to be *democracy*—John Dewey's, of course, defined as whatever the particular teacher thought it was or thought Dewey meant it to be. With such heavy dependence on individual creativity, no standard form can emerge, but many things can happen. There is a pattern.

To bring about this democratic school, each new generation of reformers comes to the conclusion that instructional programs must:

1. be adapted to the child's natural curiosity and development,

2. tie in naturally as a continuation of the child's life outside the school,

3. use social problems as the central organizer of study content,

4. select whatever specific materials of instruction can be used from the disciplines to explain the social or natural phenomena operating in the problem under study, thus constantly demonstrating the interrelatedness of all knowledge,

5. teach the basic reading, writing, and number skills as a by-product of social activity so that the child pursues these studies with interest and enthusiasm rather than simply with acquiescence.

To bring about democratic group educational experiences, logic dictates that classrooms be conducted as cooperative communities. Pupils establish rules by discussion and consensus, with the teacher participating only as an equal member of the group. Study tasks will be centered around a topic of inquiry chosen by the pupils as a group. The topic should be a social problem of immediate concern to the pupils and one within which every pupil can find a focus to apply his own personal talents or interests as a contribution to the research. The various aspects of the inquiry will be divided into projects assigned to committees. Information-gathering excursions will stimulate enthusiasm for pursuing the project. The pursuit of information will stimulate interest in basic reading skills. The desire to quantify information gathered will create an interest in learning mathematics. The necessity for reporting among committees will create the felt need to learn the basic communication skills of writing correct English. Questions of "how" and "why" will bring in scientific inquiries. All of these are to be taken up as the pupils feel a need for them, not by a preplanned schedule. The help of specialist teachers will be sought, thus bringing about an automatic integration of subject matter.

The solicitation of help from specialists requires democratic cooperation among teachers. This leads into shared responsibility for outcomes, assignments of shared responsibility for specific groups, and making flexible grouping and time allocations possible within a block of assigned time ordinarily broken up among several independent teachers. With different groups doing different things at different times, non-graded, multi-age, or ability grouping are readily possible; expanded libraries, resource centers, and learning laboratories (science, language, mathematics, etc.) become a part of the learning environment; spaces are adjusted to meet demands of previously unconventional activities. Every pupil progresses at his own rate of learning, and he feels personal satisfaction from contributing to the group project. Some type of home room assignments are made so that every pupil has a teacher who serves as guidance counselor and keeps track of his academic progress. Or so the prescription goes.

Most of these things are an unspecified part of every well taught classroom. When these aspects are named and discussed, they are labeled progressive education or humanistic education, and they become attempts to mass produce the results of the tutorial or the one-room school run by a highly talented teacher. But this highly talented teacher is now expected to be made up of several subject specialists, all functioning as one person, with knowledge of each pupil's social-emotional needs. All of the examples reviewed in the previous chapters included all of these aspects in some form. None of them are truly innovations. They have been with humanity since the beginning. They are part of every purposive human relationship. Circumstances may alter which of the aspects dominates in a specific situation, in this case, *school*, but the others are there secondarily. Although they can be diagrammed as an interrelated configuration, the presentation is too simple. The situation is more nearly analogous to the presence of all colors in white light. Sorted through a prism, the spectrum can be studied, but nothing has been removed. The sorting exists only within the prism. The prism is the key to the knowledge, which cannot be seen by the human eye in any other way, unless one waits for the occasional rainbow impossible to capture or control for analysis.

Viewing society as white light and school as a prism, school sorts the functional environment into the disciplines to be studied. The pupil then applies this knowledge in experiencing the greater society. Just as a prism is an artificial environment for light, the school is an artificial environment for social interaction. A prism does not provide a meaningful experience of light in miniature with all of the molecular relationships and possible functions brought within the grasp of the human mind. No more can a school provide a meaningful experience of society in miniature with the infinite interrelationships and possible applications simplified and brought within the grasp of the pupils' minds. As a prism sorts out colors to be studied at their point of highest intensity, leaving their interrelationship to be experienced in the totality of white light, so the school sorts out the disciplines of knowledge to be studied at their point of intensity, leaving the social interrelationships to be experienced in the totality of the greater society.

The analogy breaks down with the introduction of the fact that a human viewing light through a prism is studying a function of which human beings are not a contributing part. Humans studying social forms through a school are indeed studying themselves from several points of view, all of the while they are living the phenomena they are studying. Certainly the bandwagon terms describing types of schooling represent only a point of entry into discussion of the configuration. In any discussion, the limitations of labeling parts of social interactions must be taken into consideration. The total is always present and exerting an influence.

In talk about schooling, collective terms or different labels for the various aspects of the social relationship gain currency and appear to be clearly definable, when indeed, each one simply has been placed at the center of the discussion with the other aspects shown in their relationship to it. The starting point, it seems, can be chosen arbitrarily and if the analysis of the relationships is carried far enough, it will be found that all of the others are included in some form.

The Fund for the Advancement of Education program of the 1950s picked up labels for presumably separate innovative practices, and in the 1960s it funded programs that attempted to utilize all of them in one educational complex. In reality, the search was for administrative controls or provisions that would allow all of these practices to function to the maximum advantage of all concerned. The labels enjoying currency at the time were: 1) team teaching, 2) the use of non-professional personnel in schools, 3) flexible scheduling, 4) variable size pupil groups for instruction and new space arrangements, 5) the use of audio-visual resources, including educational television, 6) programmed instruction, 7) language laboratories, 8) educational data processing by machine, 9) independent study, 10) advanced placement and early admissions, 11) non-graded school programs, and 12) school and university partnerships for curriculum improvement, and pre- and in-service teacher preparation. These can all be talked about independently, but Whiting's example of the use of labels dispels any illusion that labels on the aspects of schooling are mutually exclusive:

It is more convenient and comfortable, for example, to describe one's school as a "team teaching school" (form) than it is to describe the same school as one in which "the varied talents, interests and backgrounds of teachers are deployed to give maximum effect in instruction, and cooperative planning and evaluation are structured into the schedule, and pupils are grouped by ability and interest to provide flexibility, etc., etc., etc. (function) [1]

This description already includes items 1, 3, 4, and 11 above, and would certainly include 2, 5, 6, 7, and 9 if the etceteras were filled in. The problem seems to be that social phenomena are clusters of relationships the form of which is in the mind of the beholder. The labels are made up of words already defined with functional implications dependent upon each person's interpretation of his own life experience. Thus labels for social phenomena are artificial divisions of an interdependent whole which cannot be sorted out and

[1] David Whiting, "Final Report on the Supplementary Grant January 1966–August 1968" (Newton, Massachusetts: Newton Public Schools, January 1970), mimeographed, p. 27.

independently controlled. They can only be grouped for flow. Science invents new names for newly discovered phenomena— electricity, laser beam—and there are no previous meanings to the words to confuse the interpretation, or which allow their application to incremental, partial, or mixed products. School is a mixed product. The new school practices encouraged by the Ford funded programs were simply different words to describe the parts of organizational patterns of schools or classrooms. New names gave the feeling that a new order had been imposed on the school program. Closer inspection reveals that it was only a new way of talking about the old order, using a different point of emphasis.

Team Teaching and Para-professionals

Team teaching by its simplest definition is shared leadership in a school or classroom or with reference to a specific group of pupils in a school. It can range in function from informal mutual agreements between or among the people concerned, to formal assignments written into the administrative governance of the school. The team teaching innovative programs of the sixties were innovative only in that the label *team teaching* was applied to them. Certainly conducting the classroom is part of the *teacher's* task. The allocation of duties to pupil helpers, teacher aides, para-professionals, teacher interns, or special teachers can be viewed as forms of team teaching. School practices that could formally be called team teaching have ranged from the simple administrative relationship of two teachers assigned to divide specific responsibilities between them to interdependent relationships involving the whole school staff including the principal and janitor.

In Parker's practice school, the presence of teacher interns, the regular teachers' responsibility for contributing to the auditorium programs, Parker's own participation in conducting the opening exercises, and his insistence on stressing the cooperative community aspects of the school experience all qualify as forms of team teaching. In Dewey's laboratory school the team teaching practices were at the same time both informal and formal and involved every level of teacher cooperation. The subject specialists were required to coordinate instruction with the topics each group teacher was working on. There were teacher interns and student researchers working with the teachers. The whole school was conceived as a cooperative community with Dewey instilling his philosophy at frequent teachers meetings.

In the Gary schools the elaborate network of formally stipulated coordination of departmentalized instruction included every form of team teaching. There were pupil helpers in the classroom. There were older pupils teaching younger ones. There were special "application" teachers assigned to coordinate scientific, dramatic, or construction activities with the theme specified by the regular group teacher. There were classrooms shared by two teachers (one more experienced to help the other). And in addition, the whole school program accommodated pupil participation in all of the tasks of running the school and maintaining the buildings and grounds.

Team teaching at the Hamilton School in Newton had a clear organizational form, but there is nothing in the term itself that dictated the specific form. The term specifies only teaching in all of its ramifications attended to by two or more people. All other details are determined by the specific people in the specific situation. The personalities and talents of the teachers involved will control the type of teaching that occurs, regardless of administrative assignments. Indeed, it is difficult to draw a sharp line between team teaching and just plain teaching.

It seems logical that a number of subject specialists, teamed to teach a total program to a group of students, could certainly present a more meaningful school experience than can be achieved with each teacher independently teaching the essence of his chosen specialty. The problem with the logic is that schooling has a traditional pattern—teachers instruct or assign, pupils listen or study. It is the simplest form of staff utilization to improve efficiency. It is the group extension of the parent child relationship. With the increase in the number of pupils in a school, efficiency is further improved with age grading in elementary schools and subject specialization in secondary schools. But through it all, the conventional classroom, with one teacher for thirty to forty pupils remains, each teacher functioning, in effect, as an independent business.

Team teaching as a formal arrangement upsets this independence of thought and action. It requires that one such teacher be put in charge of several other teachers, all expected to cooperate to schedule their teaching in a way that more pupils can benefit from highly talented teaching. Whereas ordinarily each teacher plans a program to teach the basics of a specialty, and adjusts it from day to day depending on pupil response, team teaching requires constant interaction with one or several other teachers, establishing a program adjusted by consensus, and making day to day adjustments dictated not only by one's own errors of judgment, but also by errors of judgment or failure of performance on the part of the other members of the team. In addition, the team leader's control is limited to the power of personal persuasion. The leader does not have the power to select compatible personalities for the team nor to dismiss those either unwilling or unable to adjust their teaching in accordance with a group consensus.

Each team member is, in effect, free to choose the extent to which he will cooperate. Under such constraints, a business for profit would go bankrupt very quickly, and such is the fate of all efforts at team teaching that attempt any more than simply to specify that the focus of instruction for a grade level be on a specific historical period—colonial America, renaissance Europe—or on a specific social focus—international trade, city government—leaving each teacher to his own classroom and independent selection of materials in his specialty.

Even efforts in elementary school to put two teachers (one math-science, the other social studies-English) together with a group of sixty-five pupils in a large room with movable space dividers creates counterproductive feelings of competition between the teachers. Tensions arise because pupils choose a favorite of the two, and there is no third party to insure that both contribute equally. A team leader may end up carrying responsibility for all of the planning and thinking for as many as a hundred pupils and for another teacher who is receiving equal credit for all of the team accomplishments.

Thus, team teaching or any other plan for integrated curriculum means only that the teacher no longer can simply teach as individual conscience directs, but must, in effect, merchandise all ideas and plans and justify them to the other members of the team for approval before work can proceed. There is little wonder that attempts to integrate studies are soon reduced to *live and let live* arrangements. It has been tried in many forms, from teams of two to whole schools, and the institution of school could not accommodate it as an on-going program structure.

The use of non-professionals in the classroom was tried as a means of stretching the available teacher services to reach more pupils. It was not projected that teachers would change radically, only that somehow the job could be reorganized in such a way that the removal of non-teaching organizational or clerical tasks would enable teachers to handle more pupils. It was assumed that a teacher's output could be increased by increasing class size and hiring clerical administrative assistants for such tasks as keeping registers, supervising halls, or scoring pupil written work. Unfortunately, the time spent by an assistant at these tasks does not free an equal amount of teacher time for other things as long as the self-contained classroom remains. In fact, it gives the teacher the added responsibility of supervising the assistant, and it may well remove tasks that provide a needed variation in pace and a needed pupil contact, while increasing the high pressure duties beyond a reasonable expectation of previous accomplishment. Since knowledge of pupil attendance and performance on written work provide a most important guide to lesson planning and evaluation, the teacher still has to spend time on them. And any increase in class size has to reduce the amount of attention each pupil receives from the teacher, and has to alter the quality of the teaching. If assistants are used to help with instruction, time has to be taken to instruct the assistant, and the quality of the overall instruction suffers. This is not to say that the choice to deliver a lesser product to more pupils is invalid, only that the expectation of the same quality of instruction to increased numbers of pupils by one teacher is invalid, even with the removal of clerical tasks. Such choices are justified only when economic constraints dictate them.

Flexible Scheduling, Variable Grouping, Non-Grading, Independent Study

Grouping and scheduling are so interdependent that discussing them separately lacks meaning. The normal spread in pupil age and ability in a school dictates grouping for instruction, and groups must be scheduled for the appropriate level of instruction. In the early days of the age-graded school, the whole class was instructed as a unit, using specific textbook material. Those failing to keep pace either repeated the grade or withdrew from school. Scheduling amounted only to assignment to a room for a year. In departmentally organized high schools, grouping and scheduling had to accommodate moving class groups from one room to another for different studies. Elective offerings further altered grouping and scheduling requirements. The advent of the child development studies brought a confusion of demands to meet individual pupil needs without sacrificing the fiscal economy of large schools.

Variable size grouping for special instruction has been advocated by progressive educators since the turn of the century and has become common practice in classrooms and schools in many forms. In elementary schools, art and social studies are usually whole class activities; reading instruction is usually in small groups of eight or ten. Arithmetic instruction varies from a whole class activity to independent study for exceptional pupils. Several classes are often gathered for folk dancing instruction, or for auditorium programs.

These groupings are based on age, ability, or achievement, or combinations of these factors. Deviations from age-graded classes are uncommon except in elective studies in high school. The most common alternative to age-grading is ability grouping, the ultimate of which is the totally non-graded school with each pupil on an independent progress track.

Ability grouping in some form has been a part of every program. The Dewey school sorted the intellectually oriented from the hand oriented and grouped accordingly. The Gary schools' breadth of choice resulted in a *de facto* grouping by academic or non-academic activities. Core curriculum certainly used ability grouping, some surveys showing that twenty-two per cent of the core classes were for groups labeled retarded. Many core classes were for the gifted, and almost all of the core programs were elective in some way, such as requiring parental consent, that attracted certain types of pupils and not others.

Flexible grouping for different activities was characteristic of the Parker practice school auditorium programs, class construction projects, etc. The Dewey school groups changed constantly as some needed tutorial instruction where others did not. The Gary plan, departmentalized even in the elementary grades, had flexible grouping within classes for special activities and between classes where pupils could be assigned to whatever level was appropriate in each subject.

Experimental multi-age groupings to teach social acceptance and concern for others, younger or older, have always been a part of the progressive educational innovations. Parker's daily auditorium programs certainly qualified. The Dewey school grouped for so many factors that multi-age automatically resulted in almost all of the groupings. The Gary schools had the graded basic classrooms for elementary pupils, but much of their day was spent in multi-age groupings in the gymnasium, auditorium, shops, laboratories, etc. Although the courses were graded, the pupils could be assigned according to ability or achievement in each subject, so the individual Gary pupil was not graded. Core curriculum groups were both age-graded and usually selected in accordance with other criteria, but within the class there were many other groupings for interest and ability. Theoretically core groups included the full range of ability for the purpose of teaching respect for all levels of ability to contribute.

Flexible scheduling becomes an automatic accompaniment of any variation in the school program. Variable grouping is dependent upon flexible scheduling. This is easily accomplished in elementary school with one teacher in charge of the whole program for a class. It is more difficult in the departmentalized secondary school where the scheduling of several subjects must be coordinated for a group of pupils. The Parker practice school accommodated nature walks, excursions into the community, and other activities that might interrupt a whole school day. The Dewey school constantly varied schedules as the interest or needs of a group directed. Flexible scheduling was easily accommodated in the Gary schools with the extended school day and the long periods of auditorium participation or group activity on the playground that could be interrupted for special projects. The block-of-time scheduling that became the most visible characteristic of secondary school core curriculum programs was designed to allow for part or all of the class to spend a full morning or a full afternoon away from the school, or it allowed them to stop research work and spend full time on English grammar, for instance, for a full week.

A non-graded school cannot function without both flexible scheduling and team teaching. Independent study is automatically non-graded since it is tailored to the needs of an individual's achievement in a specific field of study. And, of course, a prime consideration in all of these variations in scheduling and grouping is the fact that the materials to be learned remain graded by their very nature and must be so accommodated. There is no getting around the fact that the ability to learn higher forms of quantification, for instance, is dependent upon previous mastery of the number system and the primary number functions.

New Space Arrangements, Curriculum Reform

The problem of technological support of innovative programs—space, equipment, and up-dated materials—has been with every effort. Traditionally, a teacher controls a classroom, be it an elementary school room with the same pupils all day, or a secondary school room with different pupils each hour. Other areas such as auditoriums, gymnasiums, and yards are shared either as general use or scheduled. Innovative space arrangements include groups moving into corridors for more space, movable partitions in classrooms to divide space, movable furniture for variable use of space, and buildings specially constructed for classrooms built around a common resource and activity center. Motion pictures have become more available as instructional materials. Record players are almost universally available. Audio-visual materials centers are common to most school systems. Teaching by closed circuit television, or by programmed instructional materials on a computer is still in the experimental stage. Video-taping of teacher trainees so that they can observe themselves has proved highly effective, but expensive.

It was adjustments in space arrangements and materials of instruction that gave visibility to progressive education. Parker struggled with simply replacing tedious textbooks with more varied and appropriate materials. Printing the pupils' stories in pamphlet form to be used for reading instruction was an example of this. For variations in space arrangements, Parker's teachers roamed the countryside with their classes while conducting observation exercises and language lessons. Working with the limited resources available for relatively small numbers of pupils, Dewey similarly took up learning by doing and brought many unconventional materials and activities into the school program. Supervised excursions were necessary to augment the experiences available in the school. Art lessons were frequently in the garden. Construction projects were often done on the outside grounds of the Dewey school. Surely it can be said that the Gary plan provided for all of these contingencies with its purposely broad corridors into which classes could overflow to utilize long tables for project work, with elementary desks that had movable tops

and stools that could be carried anywhere, and with its laboratories, shops, swimming pools, libraries, and gardens.
During the core curriculum movement, several junior high
schools were designed and built on a modular plan with movable walls to provide flexible space. In many instances a core
curriculum group of a hundred was assigned to several ad-
joining rooms to be used at the convenience of the particular
project work.

School-University Partnerships

School-university partnerships have been with us ever since
the Boston Latin School started preparing boys for Harvard
in 1640, and Harvard graduates supported themselves temporarily as teachers while awaiting an opening into their
chosen professions. Not much changed until about 1840
when Horace Mann invented teacher training colleges and
demonstration schools to provide practice under master
teachers. By 1900, both of these functions were being included in universities as departments of pedagogy or schools
of education. Since then teacher education has received its
share of attention, but it has never been considered adequate
and it never will be until the task of the teacher is defined
by real rather than ideal expectations. No amount or type of
teacher education will enable teachers in schools to provide
social learning experiences appropriate to each pupil, that will
duplicate, augment, or counteract the teaching received in
the home. There is no consensus on desirable social performance or on the criteria for judging success in life, so in the
area of social education, teachers are predestined to fail in
the education of every pupil in some way. Programs to draw
more people into the teaching profession will simply draw
more people into the teaching profession. These people will
be no more highly talented than those we already have, and

they will perform the same as the teachers we already have, not as social engineers.

Since the school curriculum is geared to college preparation, the teachers are prepared with psychological learning theory and the academic disciplines even though innovative programs may ask them to solve pupil problems of hunger, rags, and lice. Nonetheless, university-school cooperation has been a sought-after part of all of the innovative programs. Parker's practice school was the training ground for students from Cook County Normal School. The Dewey school was a laboratory to test the theories of education being taught at the University of Chicago. Many of the core curriculum programs were in university laboratory schools, and all of the core programs sought the advice and guidance of university faculty members. It is even reasonable to conclude that university faculty members were the main promoters of the core curriculum concepts. In Ford's Comprehensive School Improvement Program, the teacher was viewed as the key to school improvement, but instead of taking a long, hard look at the job description, the emphasis was placed on recruiting and training better people to be teachers who would, by their own creativity, improve schools. Most of the Newton programs were carried on with the advice or full control of Harvard faculty members.

The funding of programmed instruction and language laboratories was a continuation of the on-going effort to provide more effective instructional materials for individual progress while reducing or replacing teacher supervision with newly developed technology. Actually, a textbook is a form of programmed instruction with its questions at the end of each chapter. Adding the answers for the learner to score his own responses and to decide either to repeat a similar exercise or to go on to the next lesson brought the label *programmed instruction*. Putting such materials in a computer relieves the pupil of self-monitoring. The computer chooses the next task which is either a repeated exercise or a new concept.

Language laboratories involve a slightly different application of the term *laboratory* to a collection of text and sound recorded materials for foreign language instruction, including the equipment for playing the recordings. Such facilities made foreign language instruction possible in schools too small to merit having a special teacher for the purpose.

Electronic processing of educational data was another effort to free teachers by utilizing technology. The usefulness of this has been limited, owing to the necessity for standardizing the educational data to give to the computer. Appropriate procedures have not been worked out, and may be inherently more complicated and time consuming than the circumstances merit.

7

THE POSSIBLE:
SUCCESSES AND PROBLEMS

In all of the cited programs, the successes were individual, and were subjectively evaluated. There has never been a study or controlled survey sufficiently broad in scope to determine whether the incidence of democratic thinking or social awareness of pupils in these programs was any greater than would occur as a result of parental instruction, conventional schooling, church attendance, and civic activities ordinarily a part of growing up in the United States. Evidence from social attitude questionnaires is unreliable, because it tells only that democratic social theory has been systematically taught and that the individual chose to answer the questionnaire in accordance with it. It tells nothing about whether the individual chooses to *act* in accordance with it. Observations of democratic group process in a classroom under the surveillance of a teacher must be accepted only as an exercise of expected performance, not as an independent value choice on the part of the pupils.

Basic skills instruction in these programs took place in time set aside from the activity program, and it used the traditional methods, materials, and drill. There is no real evidence that such instruction in connection with investigating a social problem is any more effective than simply good teaching in a regularly conducted classroom. There are, in fact, recorded opinions to the contrary. All of these programs had their detractors, heavily fortified with tradition, and in addition, there were those who participated and faced the facts.

The evidence was overwhelming, but admissions of shortcomings were usually couched in terms of needs—for better teacher training, more willingness to cooperate, smaller classes, production of suitable instructional materials, reliable tests of social attitudes, and objective criteria for choice of content. The implications were always that if enough people were willing to try, somebody would surely find solutions. But the answer was simple. Teachers could not do it.

Looking Back

The illusion of possibility came from a few highly talented teachers who were able to orchestrate apparently spontaneous group activity in the study of social problems. Characteristic of these programs, however, was a teacher-enforced adherence to patterns of democratic group process. Rosalind Zapf, who undoubtedly taught ideal core as nearly as it is possible for a human being to do it, admitted that in each class of thirty-five, there were probably five or six who could be depended upon to function in accordance with the ideals of democratic living, and that they were able to carry it on in their later lives only in a limited way.[1] In view of the fact that the rules of our democratic form of government are taught in all schools regardless of the form of conduct of the school, and such values instruction is, in addition, part of much religious teaching, it seems not unreasonable to expect to find this proportion of convinced democratic thinkers even without its being practiced in the school organization.

Admissions of shortcomings by zealots must certainly be given more than passing mention. Dewey admits that the

[1] Personal interview, Rosalind Zapf Pickard, August 1, 1973.

principles formed only a working hypothesis rather than a fixed schedule:

> The principles of the school's plan were not intended as definite rules for what was to be done in school. They pointed out the general direction in which it was to move. . . . As the outcome of such conditions and others such as changes in the teaching staff, equipment, or building, the "principles" formed a kind of working hypothesis rather than a fixed program and schedule. Their application was in the hands of the teachers, and this application was in fact equivalent to their development and modification by teachers. The latter had not only great freedom in adapting principles to actual conditions, but if anything, too much responsibility was imposed upon them. In avoiding hard and fast plans to be executed and dictation of methods to be followed, individual teachers were, if anything, not given enough assistance either in advance or by way of critical supervision. There might well have been conditions fairer to teachers and more favorable to the success of the experiment.[2]

Dewey further states:

> While constant conference was needed to achieve unity, . . . of course, the unity came far short of rating one hundred per cent. But experience showed that there are checks upon dispersion and centrifugal effort that are more effective than are the rigid planning in advance and the close supervision usually relied upon.[3]

Although "association and exchange among teachers" was presumably the Dewey school's substitute for supervision, and work was reputedly directed on the basis of cooperative social organization of teachers, such teachers had to be highly selected. It is unclear exactly who made the autocratic choice, but it happened:

> It soon becomes evident under conditions of genuine cooperation whether a given person has the required flexibility and ca-

---

[2] quoted in Mayhew and Edwards, pp. 365–366.
[3] quoted in Mayhew and Edwards, p. 367.

pacity of growth. Those who did not were eliminated because of the demonstration that they did not "belong"....[4]

The experience of teaching in a conventional school had been a part of the preparation of most of them, and their own educational upbringing had been full of free activity with a rich childhood experience.... All were selected as carefully as possible with reference to their social fitness, and the result seemed to suit, in a rather remarkable manner, the needs of the pupils.[5]

However:

When manual training, art, science, and literature were all taught, it was found that one person *could not* be competent in all directions, even if this had been desirable.[6]

Although an acceptable method of conducting classes gradually developed, it varied with the personality of the teacher, as did the duties of the class leader, a pupil selected daily. It was clearly admitted that the school failed to meet an expressed need by children for a grading system or objective evidence of their own advance.[7]

Since the school attracted an exclusive group of parents and pupils, the successes of these pupils may well have derived from influences other than the Dewey school experience. One pupil's recollections verify doubts as to the completeness of claimed successes, and gives a disquieting picture of a child brainwashed into acceptance of a stereotyped view of himself and his place in the world. It also reveals a possible destructive effect of the school's grouping criteria:

I never learned to spell—I do not know how to spell now, I have no sense of spelling. Of my group some were spellers and some were not. I had two sisters and a brother in the school. My

[4] quoted in Mayhew and Edwards, p. 371.
[5] Mayhew and Edwards, p. 373.
[6] Mayhew and Edwards, p. 377.
[7] Mayhew and Edwards, p. 376, 377.

brother and one sister learned to spell; the other sister and I did not. My brother was of the book type and began to read early. I was of the shop type and was not interested in books. I did not feel the need of reading or writing and hence no desire to learn to spell. There would have come a time when I would have wanted to write up what I had found out and what I was doing in the shop. Then I would have learned to spell. But the school as an experiment stopped just before we non-book people came to the point where we wanted to write or read. This was bad for the experiment and was very bad for us. . . .

I don't remember any *studying* or *learning* of anything. I don't remember going through the process of learning to read, but I read. However, I never read a book of my own free will until I reached the second year in high school.[8]

Apparently the Dewey school freed the pupils from the self-discipline required in the real world, and thereby failed to prepare them for it.

Wirt, in the Gary schools, actually provided the freedom to which Dewey only aspired. What Dewey contrived to insure by psychological control of the staff and pupils, Wirt set out to achieve by providing access to an enabling environment. The heavy criticism by the Flexner report certainly lost sight of the reality. While giving Wirt credit for providing the democratic school atmosphere recommended by Dewey, Flexner criticized severely the standards of academic performance, even though the working class children of Gary tested very near to the national norms. "Fundamentally, the defect is one of administration," said Flexner's report,[9] arguing that standards of excellence were not rigorously enough applied, and activities were not closely enough controlled. This brings into question what the standards of reference were. The people of Gary were fully pleased with their schools which were viewed as equal or superior to those considered the best in

[8] Mayhew and Edwards, pp. 404–405.
[9] Flexner and Bachman, p. 200.

the nation. But the idea was condemned by the report because the schools failed to bring their working class children to "high" levels of academic achievement, the teachers were not all equally superior, some of the teaching was "old fashioned," and classes were too large for desirable individual attention.[10] Certainly this is a description of the universal human condition as much as of the Gary schools. Nevertheless, only under the charisma of Wirt was the Gary plan able to succeed. It is reasonable to assume that Wirt was willing to opt for as much freedom as was possible within the inherent limitations of human society. Perhaps this was his genius.

Evaluations of core curriculum revealed the same criticisms. The ideal inspired imaginations, but most often, the unimaginative were assigned to accomplish it. Problems listed by administrators were:

1. The available teachers could not teach core.
2. Time for planning could not be scheduled.
3. Cooperation of other teachers could not be coordinated.
4. There were no reliable criteria for determining the actual needs and interests that were real to pupils.
5. Appropriate instructional materials and space were not available.
6. The projected outcomes were intangible and could not be evaluated.[11]
7. Classes were too large.

Aiken wrote, documenting from hindsight the problems or aspects not sufficiently accommodated in the Eight-Year Study. These, presented in brief, are: (1) willingness to innovate does not insure ability to do it; (2) highly skilled democratic leadership is absolutely necessary; (3) in a public school, leadership figures in the entire community must be

10 Flexner and Bachman, p. 202.
11 Wright (1952), pp. 42–45.

supportive; (4) the whole school must be involved in the program; (5) outside consultants are needed at least for the first several years; (6) among schools, interchange of curriculum and evaluation materials is needed for any wide-ranging program development; (7) incremental reports of progress must be widely publicized to promulgate gradual acceptance of what may grow into a radical revision of past policies, and thus may reflect on other related institutions.[12] It will be recalled that it was for failure to closely control all of these things that Wirt was so severely criticized.

Alberty reminisced, "After World War II, we participated in the hopeless task of keeping alive the movement in which we had worked for so many years." [13] Twenty-five years devoted to the promotion of core curriculum had brought nothing concrete to grasp. They had demonstrated only that highly creative and motivated teachers can conduct exceptionally productive learning environments given the time, money, and freedom. This was desirable for all, of course, but without such teachers, the programs were doomed to mediocrity.

There are several important questions intrinsic to the success of the democratic school that were left unattended in the literature on innovative schooling. Most of them relate to the problems with definition and evaluation. Since accepted conventions of human interaction can vary circumstantially or be so adjustable as to be almost subjectively determined, can such training be placed in the hands of nonspecialists? Are we not asking core teachers to function beyond real limits? How valid is the attempt to teach children to conduct themselves by a pattern of beliefs different from those held by their parents; that is, different from those de-

---

[12] Aikin (1953), pp. 11–12.
[13] Harold B. Alberty, "My Friend, 'Hank' Hullfish," *Educational Theory*, XIII (July 1963), p. 189.

monstrated in the conduct of their parents, different from what is expected or is required for acceptance or survival in their homes? How much can a teacher be expected to accomplish given the realities of our social system; that is, what are the probable outcomes as opposed to the hoped for possible achievement or the ideal? At what point, going down the list of six types of core, is special expertise on the part of teachers needed; that is, beyond observable mainstream personal and professional conduct, do teachers need special education, training, or talent without which attempts to conduct a democratic classroom are doomed to failure? How can it be judged whether a democratic classroom is being handled well enough to provide the desired leadership experiences for *all* of the pupils; that is, can democracy be allowed to function in a classroom in such a way as to leave most of the pupils taking instruction from a few of the more aggressive pupils—an experience that can be less productive than a conventional classroom for all except the leaders? Is a contrived and controlled compulsory attendance environment, such as that in a school, an appropriate circumstance for youth to experience the working of democratic group process? Can we call it democracy when a pupil does not have the option to withdraw, when all are dependent on money, which gives power, and to which access for school-age youth is not related to personal ability but to accident of birth to particular parents?

The proponents of democracy in the classroom seemed to proceed on the belief that if they involved enough people trying it in some form, the answers to these questions would emerge from pooled results of successful programs. Clearly these questions occurred in the minds of those people who discontinued core programs or elected not to try them. The descriptions amounted only to points of view, not formulas for achieving specific results. One critic, looking for substance, expressed his dismay at the accepted jargon of core promoters who described education as that which:

equips all American youth to live democratically with satisfaction to themselves and profit to society as homemembers, workers, and citizens." Analyzed, the statement yields several propositions, none novel and all widely accepted: (1) Education equips people for living, (2) universal education is essential in a democracy and a necessary concomitant of a philosophy of equal opportunity. (3) the schools of a democracy should produce responsible citizens, (4) individual happiness is a legitimate goal of free men and their institutions, and (5) people usually have occupational and civic responsibilities as well as those in the family. All in all, they are so commonplace as to be trite.[14]

The statements are, indeed, commonplace and are in terms that depict all things to all men. The problem was to put them into concrete prescriptions for action.

The few empirical studies of innovative programs revealed that the deviation from conventional programs was more theoretical than real, because the number of teachers who did it was negligible. The others taught conventional lessons in the time block set aside for innovation. Another writer expresses dismay:

As exciting and imaginative as some of these theories were, few of them were tested with any empirical rigor in public school classrooms. . . . Instead of holding whatever definition of the core they had in mind as an hypothesis to be tested, they rushed headlong into advocacy without adequate empirical support and almost no experimental intentions.[15]

[14] Mauritz Johnson, Jr., "The Rise and Fall of Life Adjustment," *Saturday Review*, XLIV (March 18, 1961), p. 46.

[15] Harvey Overton, "The Rise and Fall of the Core Curriculum," in *Schools for the Middle Years: Readings*, ed. by George C. Stoumbis and Alvin W. Howard (Scranton, Pennsylvania: International Textbook Co., 1969), p. 231.

Paul Diederich, who was heavily involved in the promotion of core, wrote in 1970 that social reconstruction's political aspects were forced upon teachers "by a few activists who never got to first base," and that the answer of experimentalist teachers to the challenge that the school build a new social order would have been that they did not have the faintest idea how to go about it. His second point was that "the dominant idea of the thirties was probably the combination of two or more fields of study into 'core courses' or 'integrated courses' " which now seems to him to have been a "thoroughly bad idea" that he hopes will not be revived. Having "embraced the notion eagerly and watched it hopefully throughout the Eight-Year Study," he was only gradually disillusioned, he says, offering the opinion that teaching subjects together "creates far more problem than it cures." He also expresses the opinion that using, for instance, a community study unit as a vehicle to "lug in" basic skills instruction in math or science or English is poor practice which serves only to detract from the importance of pursuing the community study.[16]

The only approach to a controlled experiment, the Eight-Year Study, neglected either to specify or to evaluate the most important variable, the form and quality of the innovations, the effects of which were presumably being evaluated. The nearest approach to a controlled environment example was Summerhill School, but Neill had no formal experimental structure. He just used his judgment of the pupil's needs of the moment, as a father figure, over a group that never exceeded fifty individuals. The program was A. S. Neill. Was it a democratic classroom or school? [17] It can be argued that any curriculum with outcomes dependent on teacher talent can not be classified as a program. Conducting a democratic

[16] Letter, Paul Diederich to James Squire, February 6, 1970.
[17] A. S. Neill, *Summerhill* (New York: Hart Publishing Co., 1960).

classroom activity is certainly dependent entirely on the teacher's creativity and personality. Thus, it almost seems that the core promoters over thirty years were "appraising non-events in program evaluation" or, at best, a non-program.[18]

In the context of the conclusion that the democratic classroom or school is a paradoxical concept, what do the claims of success mean? What are these teachers doing? They are doing as much as can be done in existing schools. They have adjusted the ideal to the possible. They talk about democratic ideals, conduct discussions, and enforce a superficial social tolerance in school. Beyond that, they must present the expected curriculum. The term *curriculum* as applied to school activities has a traditional and unshakeable meaning in the public mind. It is a selection or arrangement of content that will be mastered as the outcome of a teacher-directed experience. The product is clearly expected to be knowledge of content, and the job of the school is to teach content that would not otherwise be learned, or at least not as easily.

[18] W. W. Charters, Jr. and John E. Jones, "On the Risk of Appraising Non-Events in Program Evaluation," *Educational Researcher*, II, No. 11 (November 1973), pp. 5–7.

8

LESSONS OF THE PAST
NEWLY LEARNED

In summarizing the experimental programs of the Newton schools from 1960 to 1970, David Whiting was wont to label the time an "age of innocence," having found that "experimentation overcomes preconceived notions" about what can be done in schools. Newton experimented with a full range of the popular "new" concepts of school organization under several different conditions:

The opening of a new school—from scratch.

Complete reorganization of an existing school—in a number of instances—ungraded schools.

A "school within a school" organizational innovation in the existing plant—under the same roof.

A "school within a school" organizational innovation—physically separated from the parent organization.

The combining of two existing faculties into a new faculty—new principal—new building—open space concept—no walls—an interesting experiment with the "territorial imperative".

Numerous instances of new organizational patterns from redeployment of teachers and pupils within an existing graded structure—some limited crossing of grade lines by subject—cooperative teaching and departmentalization. This was the only one to enjoy considerable spin-off within the system.[1]

[1] Whiting, "Final Report, "p. 30.

In looking back over the "age of innocence" he recalls that at the beginning:

many of us assumed . . . that we knew where salvation lay if we could just get our hands on the muscle, defined as money. *And where did salvation lie? Surely, it was in curriculum reform and organizational change.* Curriculum reform would replace the compromising mediocrity of the textbook editor with the rigor of scholars and the honesty of original sources, the talk and chalk pedantry so prevalent in the best of school systems with the best of Brunerian theory, the institutionalized arrogance of the formal curriculum guide with the correctional insurance of field testing in the classroom. Organizational changes would begin to dismantle the egg-crate school in administrative practice and teaching strategy if not in bricks and mortar. And though somewhat less sure of ourselves here, we would even underwrite some effort in that most sensitive of domains, the everyday classroom tactics of the teacher.

I recall it as a period of genuine optimism . . . [anticipating] "great leaps forward." . . .[2]

The central thrust of this cluster of organizational projects was an attempt to unlock the lockstep aspects of elementary and junior high education. The Hamilton, Horace Mann and Meadowbrook [non-graded] programs were and are of this type. The N.S.E.P. at Newton South High School was a "school within a school" attempt to shake loose the high school structure and reduce the adversary relationships of faculty and students.[3]

These examples focused on the organizational aspects of schooling, making changes that were expected to free pupils and teachers to work creatively with content. Such efforts are often criticized for attending only to form and ignoring content. It must be recognized that the one-teacher classroom with conventional rows of desks is simultaneously frustrating and reassuring or confirming. For example, since swimming

---

[2] Whiting, "Final Report," p. 5.
[3] Whiting, "Final Report," p. 21.

instruction cannot be construed as a classroom activity, its absence from the curriculum is fully defensible. When desks must be moved aside in order to include an active game, the game can be defensibly viewed as inappropriate for classroom instruction, although less so. The walls and furniture lend security to the job. They almost define it.

The Newton experimental programs were described as "bold, pervasive, and very trying enterprises." [4] "Bold and pervasive" because the total school approach was used; "very trying" because the added demands were overwhelming for most teachers. Thoughtful reading of the problems as described gives the feeling that much of what is attributed to failure of sensitivity, or failure of diplomacy, on the part of administrators is more accurately attributable to the general level of talent available to the teaching profession. The plan, itself, was unreal. To the simple job of the classroom teacher has been added the confusion of constantly checking with other teachers on schedules, materials, and pupil programs. This consumes so much time and energy that there is little left even for conventional teaching to say nothing of the creative activities the new organization has presumably freed these teachers to carry out. Overriding all else, it became clear that successes were partial, that organizational change does not insure better instruction and may create more problems than it solves, and that radical variations from the traditional curriculum are possible only by a very few highly talented teachers.

In reviewing the programs in Newton, Whiting reports:

Particularly, it is impossible to apply the generalized term of excellence to the specific situations of 18,000 different pupils and their parents. This is a large heterogeneous school system and the variables are too many. . . .[5]

4 Whiting, "Final Report," p. 21.
5 Whiting, "Final Report," p. 11.

And so most of the major projects seem to fall into the barrel of qualified successes each with its own catalogue of special successes and failures within its own developmental patterns.[6]

With a charmingly mixed metaphor, "all that glittered was not innovation," the report introduces explanations of some of the redundancies that come up when schooling is thought of in terms of form and function:

It is more convenient and comfortable, for example, to describe one's school as a "team teaching school" (form) than it is to describe the same school as one in which "the varied talents, interests and backgrounds of teachers are deployed to give maximum effect in instruction, and cooperative planning and evaluation are structured into the schedule, and pupils are grouped by ability and interest to provide flexibility, etc., etc., etc." (function) . . .

More and more, it apparently becomes easy to assume that the presence of the form assures continued implementation of the function. Form is relentlessly proselytized and defended. Teacher turnover erodes the original cadre who understood the most precious concerns and functions of the program. . . .[7]

Function begins to serve form until the point is reached . . . where the more awkward and trying aspects of function that clash with formalisms are eliminated or ignored. . . . first considerations [having been] buried beneath the rhetoric about form.[8]

Here function has been described not in terms of pupil activities, but in terms of the teacher's skills and talents that are expected to be applied to the task.

Cooperative teaching was another label:

Cooperative teaching was, in a sense, an attempt to combine the best of team teaching with the best of the self-contained classroom . . . In order to retain the best of both worlds, it was

[6] Whiting, "Final Report," p. 13.
[7] Whiting, "Final Report," p. 27.
[8] Whiting, "Final Report," p. 26.

absolutely crucial to formally schedule a significant amount of team planning and team evaluation time into the schedule and this was not always accomplished.[9]

Thus, these labels, *cooperative teaching* or *team teaching*, produced an identifiable form that was easy to set up. Controlling the outcomes proved to be another matter entirely:

Originated in the Oak Hill elementary school, the plan had appeal and spread quickly. The original structure and intent survived the first spin-off to five other schools but became eroded and altered to a significant degree during the middle 60s, as the program or parts of it spread to approximately 15 other schools in the system.

It is at this point that analysis gets tricky and loaded with variables. Some people recall some negative effects in what they saw as the "pell mell push to change". Some have said that "the farther cooperative teaching spread, the less it looked like the original article". This is true, but the reasons are not singular nor entirely clear. Some of the changes were adaptations to local school conditions. Some of the Newton programs were certainly influenced by what the staff was seeing and reading about around the country in the popular press and professional literature, for it was indeed a popular movement and was being touted by some as the answer to sputnik and the knowledge explosion. . . .

To many people interviewed, the unfortunate development of this period of spin-off was that the *regularly scheduled team planning* was sloughed off in many schools and the resulting product began to look more and more like junior high school departmentalization and less and less like elementary school cooperative teaching.[10]

The core curriculum literature all carries the warning that the whole school must be involved in the experimental change or there will be problems. Newton tried partial programs anyhow and was forced to conclude:

[9] Whiting, "Final Report," pp. 23–24.
[10] Whiting, "Final Report," p. 23.

There are some indications from our experience . . . that, all other things being equal, certain structures have in them the seeds of success and others of failure or at least portents of an unbearable level of stress. . . . For example, a "school within a school" style of innovation, if housed under the same roof tends to be divisive and counter-productive. . . . The notion of two organizations, under one roof, in each other's way, constantly rubbing shoulders until everyone's shoulders are raw and bleeding, has on close examination an absurdity about it that just wouldn't be tolerated or even attempted by ordinary mortals. . . .

There sits the new offspring, . . . a repudiation . . . of the parent organization, competing for funds, teacher talent, the best of students. Around it huddles the old school tie, tongues clucking and hackles rising.[11]

And even where the total school approach was used, they apparently failed to provide adequate support for the curriculum reform that the ungraded school was expected to produce, or teachers would not have felt the need for a place to "hide," as implied:

The more radical organizational changes such as ungradedness, if carried out thoroughly and sincerely, *were and are the most wrenching,* taxing and threatening to the staff and the most pervasive and all encompassing, affecting teaching strategy, curriculum, pupil adjustment, community relations, the whole game. As one administrator puts it, "A teacher can cunningly shut off curriculum reform at her classroom door, but when a school is genuinely ungraded, there is no place to hide." [12]

Paralleling the Eight-Year Study outcomes, the Newton experience provided indications that not only the whole school, but the whole school system must be involved if a change is to have the desired effect:

In retrospect, one valid criticism that might be made of the ungraded continuous learning schools is that they are out of phase

---

11 Whiting, "Final Report," pp. 28, 29.
12 Whiting, "Final Report," p. 25.

within the system. Hamilton and Horace Mann fed into conventional junior high and high schools, and Meadowbrook is midway in a feeder system in which elementary and high school experiences are significantly different from those at Meadowbrook. A check of your files will show that the September 30, 1960 proposal for the comprehensive grant emphasizes a "campus" or "complex" on the south side of the city in which school organizational innovation would be instituted K-12, insofar as possible.

There were, at the time, formidable arguments in terms of system-wide staff and community morale against pouring a lion's share of effort into the affluent south side of the city, and the final form of our proposal in December 1, 1961 reflected somewhat the impact of these arguments by a change in emphasis. Foundation funds were to be used for oganizational innovation but on a system-wide basis in those places where forward-looking people and programs were already visible or becoming visible, regardless of location. There was still considerable interest in the Oak Hill, Meadowbrook and South High plans but a tightened K-12 sub-system was not to be. . . .

I do believe, however, that if we could have this one back again, in 1970, we might well opt for s sub-system.[13]

The lessons from the Newton experiments which were believed at the time to be successful, taught that good curriculum development:

—Takes time and money,
—Is always the art of the possible—a compromise with limited resources,
—Requires the cooperative efforts of classroom teachers and curriculum specialists,
—Takes planning and structure with ample opportunities to ad lib and improvise,
—Strongly suggests the contributions of the best scholars where feasible—this is not at all a prohibitive expense,
—Requires field testing of materials, often, piece by piece,
—Requires a thoughtful balance between prescriptions and options, recipes and open-ended materials,

13 Whiting, "Final Report," p. 22.

—Means putting useful materials in the hands of teachers and children as quickly as feasible,

—Requires self-control to avoid biting off more than you can chew,

—Takes equal self-control to blow the whistle on over-development, known as "falling in love with your own refinements",

—Means avoidance, no matter how intriguing, of exotic subject matter vehicles for which there is little material available, known as "painting one's self into a corner"—suggests backing off and taking the second option,

—Proves we can do better, in selected areas, than publishers producing for a national market,

—Revealed the weaknesses of curriculum development by solitary toilers at one extreme and cumbersome committees at the other,

—Revealed a very powerful curriculum development model—a researching, teaching, writing, materials development team—two or more talented persons attending full time to the total development task—in close contact with the teachers in the schools.

Our failures and continuing problems even with basically successful programs center around some of the following:

—The necessity to cycle limited resources among the disciplines,

—The role confrontation of teachers and curriculum specialists which always has the potential of drifting into an adversary situation,

—The problem of turnover, aggravated by role rigidity in the system,

—The problems of good conceptual development and the difficulty of evaluating this—the allure of content,

—The growing controversy over planned versus ad hoc curriculum and, amongst the planners, wide differences of opinion on the amount of prescription,

—People problems that are neglected only at peril of the effort,

—The need for integration of curriculum development and teacher training.[14]

[14] Whiting, "Final Report," pp. 48–49.

Specific mention of curriculum change problems deals almost entirely with the failure of *teachers* to follow through on recommendations. Echoing the conclusions of the core curriculum experience and its predecessors, the problem was not unwillingness, but inability on the part of teachers to constantly create curriculum for ever fluctuating pupil groups. Human beings cannot meet this demand. Whiting keeps returning to the most important factor of any curriculum—teacher talent. Certainly this is not a new insight, but his willingness to accept teacher talent for what it is—an uncontrollable variable—is a message the educational community has refused to receive from repeated past failures. The following excerpts actually summarize not only the Newton experience, but all that has gone before.

Curriculum reform efforts focused mostly on social studies-English combinations:

These system-wide social studies and science efforts, together with the English II, III, IV project, a scheme for upgrading high school English and social studies offerings for the non-college bound youngster, formed the core of curriculum reform efforts.[15]

Many of the prescriptions were impossible of accomplishment:

Here and there, . . . a dearly held myth bit the dust and we would hope that they are not resurrected in the 70s. . . .[16]

There is the gap between elementary generalists and secondary specialists with regard to the prescriptive elements in curriculum packages. . . .[17]

The reality is that the act of teaching and learning, by definition, molds the curriculum, often in quite fundamental ways. The teachers are the gatekeepers. . . .[18]

[15] Whiting, "Final Report," p. 32.
[16] Whiting, "Final Report," p. 32.
[17] Whiting, "Final Report," p. 37.
[18] Whiting, "Final Report," p. 34.

Curriculum building is always the art of the possible.[19]

Talented leadership gives a false impression of what is possible in the average school, and ignores the needs of the average teacher:

The problem is with the talented people who are naturally chosen for curriculum policy committees and project teams. The problem with these talented folk is just that, that indeed they are talented . . .[20] and they tend to structure their curriculum efforts with their own capabilities in mind. . . . That rare bird, the first-year teacher who is a natural talent, ought to be recognized for what she really is, the exception that proves the rule. . . .[21]

Initial anticipation and excitement followed by too little and/or too late with materials tends to erode confidence.[22]

Talented personnel move on to new projects, leaving behind, almost surely, reversions to *school as usual*:

The problem of transference of technique, not to mention enthusiasm, from original project cadre to new teachers, is the bane of many a promising and well endowed effort. It just may be that any project that ties its destiny too closely to the power of one or two teachers is sowing the seeds of its own demise. . . .[23]

The excitement, enthusiasm and notoriety attendant on the grants attracted some top-notch talent to Newton and gave opportunities for emergent talent within the system to surface and develop. Conversely, a considerable amount of good talent was lost to other institutions and agencies as people, made visible by our activities, responded to attractive offers. . . .[24]

We are gradually coming to realize that we have to learn to cycle talented people through the system if we expect to keep

[19] Whiting, "Final Report," p. 33.
[20] Whiting, "Final Report," p. 27.
[21] Whiting, "Final Report," p. 38.
[22] Whiting, "Final Report," p. 39.
[23] Whiting, "Final Report," p. 40.
[24] Whiting, "Final Report," p. 11.

them, giving them an opportunity at a variety of roles, and to develop system-wide flexibility and acceptance of this kind of constant movement.[25]

If school offerings are to be consistent, they must be based on tangible materials of instruction with objective means of evaluation:

There is nothing about suggested teaching procedures and sample lesson plans that need inhibit the talented experienced teacher. . . .[26]

Somehow, curriculum planners must find the magic formula for keeping teachers' attention focused on the big ideas. . . . The magic formula may just be a lot more hard work. . . .

Not all teachers share the enthusiasm of curriculum planners for the Brunerian analysis of children's learning in which the assumption is that, in effect, any idea can be taught to any child at any age, provided the exposure is appropriate. [They ask] "So what?", which simply questions the need or utility of some ideas at an early age. . . .

Though concepts and the broader understandings are what we say we are teaching toward, we don't yet even have good subjective guidelines for measuring them. . . .

Practical, rule of thumb methods for measuring concept acquisition in the classroom look to be one of the very most important tasks of curriculum development in the 70s. They won't come primarily through pencil and paper tests but through the sensitizing of teachers to the interactions going on in their own classrooms.[27]

The talented zealot can inspire enthusiasm for sweeping reforms, but even the most dedicated of teachers attempting to accomplish it simply wear themselves out.

As this has been our experience in Newton, so has it been the general experience around the country. Analyses of the recent

25 Whiting, "Final Report," p. 41.
26 Whiting, "Final Report," p. 38.
27 Whiting, "Final Report," pp. 42–44.

history of educational change reveal over and over again that the touchstone of change is the vision, drive, persuasive power and even past accomplishments of the individual innovator or of the talented staff of a school or division. . . .

During the period from 1962–1968, Hamilton's absentee rate from illness was the highest in the city while the rate of teacher turnover was the lowest, in each case by a considerable margin. Behind the rhetoric on change and innovation, lie the homely human factors of fatigue and dedication.[28]

These Newton experiences confirm previous conclusions on the problems of trying to change schools. In brief, they found that even when successful, the experience can be wrenching for the participants. It takes a strong and sensitive leader to inspire and facilitate the needed adjustments and to maintain interest. Parents must be involved in the planning. The form can be recognizably achieved with grouping and scheduling procedures, but the desired changes in function or content offered may not occur, because they are unavoidably determined by individual teacher talent. Radical organizational changes are not readily imitated, nor do they remain very long.

The overall effects, system-wide, of having experimental programs in Newton were similar to those of other times. People were stimulated, excited, and enthusiastic about doing new things. It moved the system forward and raised the sights of everyone involved. The notoriety and visibility attendant on the grants sharply increased the vocational mobility of persons. Schools not receiving special funding were negatively affected and took no interest in the innovations. The ideas were not generally picked up by non-funded schools. The terms success and failure are too simplistic to describe outcomes. Problems were in the area of planning and structure, not in spirit or intent.[29] The inevitable and rapid reversions

[28] Whiting, "Final Report," pp. 51–52.
[29] Whiting, "Final Report," p. 19.

to *school as usual* give rise to the belief that *school as usual* is what happened quietly in most of the classrooms, even during the experimental programs, similar to what Goodlad reported, much to his distress, in *Behind the Classroom Door.*[30]

As social institutions function, accomplishment of principles is approximate. Prescriptions are structured in terms of what, in somebody's opinion, *ought* to exist. Unlike physical scientists who must prove that others can do what their theories prescribe, educational theorists, like philosophers, are free to saturate the literature with utopian plans, and to insist that all could be accomplished if teachers could be induced to care enough. When dedicated teachers, like the physical scientists, prove that the task is impossible as prescribed, these teachers are accused of withholding vitally needed opportunities from children. In truth, the past hundred years of concentrated efforts have proved that the educational theorists have failed of rigor in assessing the practicability of their recommendations.

[30] John I. Goodlad and Associates, *Behind the Classroom Door* (Worthington, Ohio: Charles A. Jones Publishing Co., 1970).

9

A LIMITED SOCIAL DEBT

The problems of school reformers are problems of language. The word school itself is difficult to define. In objective terms it can be said that school is a building in which a teacher and pupils gather. The building and the people in it can be seen and touched. In subjective or purposive terms, it is often said that school is preparation for life. Unfortunately this implies that school can teach what life has to offer, and this then involves justifying school activities in terms of the meaning of life—a concept with which every person must make peace individually. School reformers repeatedly lose sight of this reality, and try to find language to describe the meaning of school, only to find themselves lost in a sea of terms equally as non-specific as life.

Criticisms—True but Not Valid

Considering school as it is known today, the recurring criticisms of it gain power because they are undeniably true. However, regardless of their truth, most of these criticisms are not valid. Any efforts to fulfill their implied demands are doomed to failure. As an hypothetical extreme to illustrate the point, it can be stated that schools teach children to hop, to skip, to jump, and even to swim, but schools fail to teach children to fly. The statement is true, but pointless.

Schools must function within the limitations of human beings. In the less obvious cases, the undeniable truth of statements so structured tends to veil or obscure the utopianism of the underlying implication that the circumstance can be remedied and that it calls for a remedy. These criticisms demand, in effect, that inherently unequal human beings be rendered equal by the school, and that the shortcomings of all other social institutions be compensated for by the school. An analysis of some of the commonly heard criticisms will explain the absurdity.

Schools fail to teach the three Rs. This is true. However, it is true only if teaching is defined in terms of forcing people to learn. An individual's circumstances and talent govern what is learned. Schools do not. Teachers cannot teach pupils who do not come to school. Teachers cannot teach pupils who come to school unprepared either socially or emotionally to cope with the confinement and stresses of school. Teachers cannot provide pupils with an incentive to learn. Teachers cannot insure that every pupil will reach a specified level of literacy. The instructional materials are presented. A pupil must choose to work to learn reading, writing, and arithmetic. Much of it has simply to be memorized. Some pupils do the work to learn, and some do not. In the final analysis, nobody can teach anybody anything. People learn.

Schools fail to teach social-emotional adjustment. This is true. An individual's life circumstances shape social-emotional adjustment. Schools do not. Teachers are not specialists in conducting group therapy sessions, and even if they were, such activity is deemed by many to be inappropriate to school. Teachers can neither choose nor dictate what pupils will believe as a result of schooling, or what social-emotional orientation will serve them best. Social attitudes are inconsistent, fluctuating, non-universal, and unmeasurable. Specific standards of behavior may be required in one set of circumstances and considered absurd by the same people in another set of circumstances. Individuals or groups can act in accordance with whatever social attitude provides the greatest immediate gain in a particular situation. Circumstances alter the way social attitudes are conformed to by a group, and an individual can choose to accept the consequences of nonconformity. Labels for social attitudes or social interaction are subject to broad interpretation owing to the imprecision of language—its inability to reflect beliefs. Language can only structure ideologies, and although social attitudes can be labeled democratic, authoritarian, selfish, or humanitarian, the individual motivation to act in a way that appears to fall into one of the categories cannot be determined. An individual's ability to recite the language patterns can be tested. An individual's actions can be observed to fulfill the expectation of a particular ideology in the opinion of the observer. This, however, cannot be looked upon as conclusive evidence that belief in the ideology controlled the action. It can only be said that the person's self-interest of the moment was served by the action observed.

Schools fail to meet the needs of all children. This is true. The greater society offers an unlimited variety of life experiences. Schools do not. Schools meet the needs of some children but not others. Teachers are not all-wise and do not pretend to be. Teachers can neither determine the varying needs of every child in a class, nor can they produce, on demand, what every child or parent thinks is needed any more than those same parents provide, on demand a different menu for each member of a family at dinner. Depending upon family background, every child is differently prepared to function in school. School serves some children better than others. Teachers cannot compensate for the difference in performance caused by varying degrees of incentive to learn. The child who learns from hearing something once will learn everything. The child who learns after hearing a hundred repetitions will learn only those things heard a hundred times. The child who learns only after a thousand repetitions is going to learn comparatively less. Lifetimes are finite. The school cannot change this. There is also no universal agreement as to how much is enough for schools to teach a child, nor could there be any way to decide when that specific amount had been learned, or whether a particular pupil had learned it in school.

Schools fail to provide equal opportunity for every child. This is true. Socio-economic status and individual talent control opportunity. Schools do not. Equal opportunity has been interpreted to mean not that all children be given access to the same books and certified teachers, but that the school must find a way to accommodate for socio-economic differences such that all pupils benefit equally from the school offering. The thinking behind this is that the disadvantaged will receive enough extra attention to insure their satisfactory performance. Applied conversely in its extreme, however, this interpretation of equality could exclude from school those children who learn a great deal from highly talented parents. They already would know as much as the school could insure that every child would learn. School cannot be expected to compensate for human or societal inequalities. It can only accept all pupils into the standard program.

Schools fail to teach the whole child. This is true. All of our social institutions collectively attend to the whole child. Schools do not. Certainly the whole child comes to school, bringing all of the complexities of human existence, only one of which is intellectual capacity. But teachers are not psychiatrists, doctors, family counselors, social workers, or all-provident parents. These roles must be filled by appropriately trained or designated people apart from the school. Teachers cannot compensate for conditions or influences external to the school regardless of how well a teacher may understand them or how limiting these conditions may be on the function or outcome of schooling for a particular child.

Schools fail to prepare adequately for life. This is true. The circumstances into which an individual is born govern the adequacy of that person's preparation for life. Schools do not. Teachers are not all-powerful guardians of the collective welfare. Teachers cannot provide the rules for the good life, because opinions differ as to what constitutes the good life. Schools cannot prepare for life, because what life offers to each individual is different, and it remains unknown until after the life has been lived. School does not define the outer limits of the use of information offered. These limits are determined by the heredity and total life experience of the individual.

Schools fail to bring about a better social order. This is true. Political pressures change the social order. Schools do not. Teachers are not politicians or social engineers. Teachers cannot instill values or specific social attitudes different from those that coincide with the social experience of the pupil. School time need not be spent on social values beyond reviewing their function and ideological structure. Attempts to teach social values at variance with those of the pupils' immediate family or society have consistently met with failure. The pupils memorize and recite the language the same as they do the alphabet. Teachers cannot control how information is used or the direction any resulting change in behavior might take. Pupils' out-of-school conduct is unalterably governed by whatever is required for survival in family and community.

Schools fail to teach children to think and act democratically. This is true. Societal constraints govern democratic thought and action. Schools do not. Teachers are not democratic leaders or social engineers. They do not preside over miniature democracies in which pupils can experience ideal social interaction while enjoying the process of discovering bits of the cultural heritage. The contention of the school reformers was that certainly if schools were run as miniature democracies, pupils would experience ideal democracy, recognize its advantages, and become ideal democratic-thinking-and-acting citizens.

Is this possible? With reference to social institutions, a thing is possible only if enough people choose to get together and make it happen. By the very nature of human beings, the ideal of democracy is impossible, because it depends on a complete meeting of minds on rules that govern—total acquiescence to a single set of rules for governance of human conduct, with each person applying the rules to himself. It could happen only if human beings were absolutely equal, physically and intellectually, and came into the world understanding and agreeing with the rules in advance. Obviously, teachers cannot conduct a democratic school or classroom regardless of how appealing the idea may sound to school reformers. Democracy as it functions among human beings is a pattern of political pressures—a give and take. Pupils are not at school to exercise political pressures to coax out an education from or for the group, or to compete with the teacher for authority. The democratic choice is always a compromise of privilege, and it includes the freedom to choose not to participate, which is paradoxical to the purpose of going to school.

Societally Mandated Schooling

In the United States there is universal free public schooling written into the laws. Every child not only has a right to schooling, but is required to attend either the tax-supported public school or an equivalent. Thus, the provision of a public school by the community is compulsory, and attendance by children approximately age six to sixteen is compulsory. This is as far as the law can go under our social organization —a government elected by the people at large, inherently unequal human beings—in an economic system based on free enterprise capitalism. Thus, the amount of schooling to be distributed at public expense to all individuals is a matter of economic expedience decided by those whose personal endowments enable them to command both wealth and the political respect of the majority. Under these conditions society can provide only equal instruction in the institution school. It cannot insure that all pupils will benefit equally, because it cannot adjust for the human individual and social inequalities of either the pupils or their parents.

Free public schooling also involves political considerations. Private schooling is a straightforward business contract. The private school controls what is offered, and pupils contract to receive it. In the case of public schooling, it is, at best, a master and servant relationship. By virtue of the fact that the community provides the building and hires the teacher, community politics can dictate what the offering is expected to be. If imaginations are allowed enough freedom, realities are obscured, and the possibilities are viewed as limitless. The community makes the unreal demands already listed. When the teachers fail to deliver, they must be inspired, trained, or replaced, goes the thinking. But the concept of school, itself, constrains. The teacher can only contrive the form of presentation. Teachers, on the whole, accomplish this task, while imposing the social regimentation necessary to get the exercises done in a sufficiently orderly way that the pupil who works can learn. That becomes the school experience of the pupils.

The intangibles in school programs become apparent when the discussions revolve around the labels form and function. Form includes the buildings, governance, and materials of instruction. Function refers to the teacher supervised activities of pupils. To say either that form follows function, or that function follows form fails to include a third influence, teacher talent—the creativity of the teacher in planning and presenting the activities. With this inclusion, function becomes the outcome of teacher talent applied to form. Only the external pattern or plan can be observed or described. Each pupil experiences it in a different way. Function is thus partially intangible, and being dependent on teacher talent, it is, for all practical purposes, impossible to prescribe in any degree of accuracy.

To the extent that society in general demands and lives up to specific levels of conduct, so will school function at those levels of conduct. Society has created and defined school. Society provides the wherewithal to accomplish school to serve its purposes. Society allocates only the minimum personnel and resources necessary to achieve school. As society defines school, the people who run schools will be able only to achieve school. Performance will remain at the point where anything less or different would be *not school*, and anything added would be more than school. Mass production of school brings organizational changes, but teaching remains the same—dependent upon individual talent. Under the tutelage of talented persons, pupils receive more than school, but such talent cannot be uniformly offered, so cannot be written into the prescription. Pupils in Gary received more than school, not by virtue of teacher talent alone, but by virtue of the fact that Wirt built total cultural complexes which made directly available to pupils many activities that were other than school, or not school. For example, a foundry on school property does not redefine foundry as school, nor does it add foundry to the definition of school. It simply provides easy access to a foundry for extended learning experiences. Providing a place for children to gather and do as

they please is certainly not school, even though school buildings and time may be used for this purpose. One cannot
include recess in the meaning of school any more than one
can include coffee break in the meaning of work.

A Controlled Environment

School is a controlled environment. Its purpose is to provide access to information supplementary to that provided
by the family, church, and other social institutions. The singleness of purpose frames the rules of order. The school is by
nature autocratic. The teacher is in charge, and is responsible
to a principal who is similarly in charge. There is content to
be learned. All pupils must be able to hear the teacher, so
classrooms must be orderly. Tests must be given, exercises
must be written until the pupil demonstrates ability to use
the information, or apply it.

Whether the pupil meets with only one teacher during a
day or with ten teachers during a day, each unit encounter
is the same. Whether the environment is a room, a swimming pool, or a nature walk, the primary form still prevails.
There is little a teacher can do to deviate from the conventional ways of presenting the symbols and patterns that must
be remembered or practiced. The pupil must be asked to
attend them often enough that shape, sound, and function
are fixed in the memory. Principles governing systematic applications must then be memorized, and exercises on these
skills supervised until the pupil can draw on the skills to
enrich daily life. Traditional school represents the minimum
practical solution to the problem. A pupil can listen to only
one teacher at a time, but a teacher can instruct as many
pupils as can come close enough to hear. Innovations that
make it possible for a teacher to instruct more pupils at a
time more effectively, have readily become part of the school

pattern. Paper and pencils for written work solve the problem of too little time for individual recitations. Graded textbooks prepared by scholars enable any teacher, regardless of talent, to present sequentially consistent lessons with little preparation. Opinions of progressive educators notwithstanding, the use of a textbook in a conventional classroom accomplishes everything that can be objectively measured in most disciplines, and accomplishes it with the least interpersonal stress. Age-graded classrooms reduce the demand on the teacher to one lesson per subject per day, more or less, and thus increase the number of pupils that can be taught by one teacher with no increase in expended energy. Workbooks to go with the textbooks further reduce demands on the teacher for lesson preparation.

Honest men may differ as to the merits of these instructional arrangements and materials as a replacement for the one-to-one tutorial, but there is no question that the economies of time and energy bring a better quality of instruction to many more children, and also enable teachers to group pupils for individual differences in development. As unsatisfactory as this may appear if judged in terms of a total educational program for the individual, if judged in terms of what can be practically accomplished in school, it is what can be offered as schooling.

A Source of Information

The traditional course of study is the culture's accumulation of logically organized symbolic subject matter presented in such a way that every child is exposed to the total picture, leaving each to benefit as individual maturity permits. This is as much as can be done equally for every child in the limited time and control allocated to school. The human beings available to be teachers can do it. At least part of the outcome can be objectively tested and clearly accepted as learned in school and unlikely to have been learned otherwise.

For functional purposes, the problem becomes one of defining the tasks of the school in terms of measurable outcomes. The only truly measurable outcomes are facility with reading, writing, and ciphering, and factual knowledge of the cultural heritage, all of which can be accomplished as functions of memory alone. Can the pupil produce the sounds represented by written words? Can the pupil produce in writing the words he hears spoken? Can the pupil read and write number symbols and perform the basic functions of addition, subtraction, multiplication, and division? When a pupil can do these things, the pupil has the basic tools with which to acquire a greater knowledge of the cultural heritage from documents. The extent of this knowledge is infinite (from the point of view of an individual's access), and there is no universally agreed upon starting point or area of primary concern that can be viewed as the primary task of the school. So beyond the basic skills, schools are left to choose the information to be delivered. Inclusion in schooling of the application of basic skills, beyond ordinary community life, to the disciplines of organized knowledge is part of the task, but it becomes more and more dependent on teacher talent, and less and less commonly offered, as the focus of inquiry becomes more specialized.

When schools venture into the realm of social attitudes or values instruction, security disappears, unless it is made clear to teachers and pupils alike that values are personally held, and that discussion of a particular social attitude does not mean it is universal or ought to be. In any structured experience of social interaction, of which school is one, the task is to sort out the aspects that can be controlled, and leave the remainder of the influences for the individuals to sort out as their abilities and life experiences permit.

With terms as seemingly straightforward as reading and writing, the simple outcomes can be extended in increasingly diffuse language to an expectation of total socialization or indoctrination. It can be argued that being able to read correctly the words from a printed page is only part of reading instruction; that included also is the ability to understand the material being read, to integrate it into one's own thought processes, to differentiate between good and bad literature, to develop a preference for good literature, and to use it as a basis for putting together one's own thoughts and formulating one's own philosophy of life. Writing can similarly be extended into what has come to be known as language arts. These extensions can be discussed by teachers and pupils in school, but any action by the pupils will be based on each individual's interpretation of the discussion.

The assumption that pupils will choose to act democratically if given the opportunity in school is unfounded in experience. The social pressures that inspire democratic choices do not exist in school. The teacher is trained, chosen, and paid to be in charge. If a teacher decides to inform pupils of the democratic ideology and to oversee pupils conducting the class accordingly, that in itself is an autocratic choice on the part of the teacher, and in most instances the pupils have had no voice in the selection of the teacher. Thus, any democratically run social institution cannot justifiably be called a school. To prescribe a democratic school is to prescribe a paradox.

The progressive school reformers were thorough. With singleness of purpose and total dedication, they worked and reworked definitions in search of words that would give clear directions to teachers who could then transform the school into a place where pupils had control of their relationships to society and of their individual destinies, instead of submitting to a program fixed in advance by the teacher. Large unit experimental programs were funded and set up where the teacher was assigned to serve as catalyst to pupil decision making, instead of as planner and assigner of tasks. It was tried not in just a few places, but in many; not with general attention to theory, but with every detail of the process listed and appropriate action prescribed; not by a few assigned teachers, but by many, fully dedicated to the task.

Teachers were unable to create such an environment, nor is it reasonable to expect that they would generally choose to do it if they could, nor is it certain that such a school experience would be beneficial for the pupils. It could even defeat the purpose of school, because outside of the school building there is the far-from-ideal society where pupils spend at least eighty-seven per cent of their time. Neither is it helpful for teachers to conduct time-consuming meetings bringing together suggestions from pupils to structure school activities in accordance with them, only to find that the final outcome, conforming to the purposes of school, coincides with standard practice manuals.

Certainly the schools should be given the assets to offer all children more information as the wealth of cultural knowledge increases, but the assignment must be limited to what is possible within the constraints of school. It is true that socialization occurs in school, but it occurs as a consequence of the gathering of human beings. It is ancillary to the purpose of school, not part of the purpose to be controlled. Thus, in spite of their thoroughness, the progressive school reformers failed to alter the actual functioning of school. Over the years, the physical appearance of school changed along with many other things in society. Buildings are substantial, well lighted, and comfortably heated. Instructional materials are relatively plentiful, attractive, and graded or sequenced for easy selection. Teachers are college educated and professionally trained. Free schooling has expanded from four years of primary instruction in the three Rs in 1860 to twelve years of primary and secondary instruction with several hundred course offerings in some of the urban high schools of today.

Yet, school, itself, has not changed. The attempted transformation did not happen. What the progressive school reformers did change was the way people talked and thought about school and about the experiences pupils have in school. The emergence of psychology as a field of study brought better general understanding of the pressures inherent in social interaction. However, applying these insights to school, the progressives were not satisfied with simply understanding the pressures inherent in school and accommodating them. Instead, they challenged the school to control social forces that are inherently uncontrollable, whether in school or in the greater society. In so doing, they extended public expectation far beyond reality.

The movements to meet the challenge were led and documented by highly talented professional educators, but language that communicated effective action could not be found. The documents remain, in monumental quantities, as a tribute to a residing belief in the perfectibility of man. School remains in its basic form—pupils performing tasks assigned and supervised by a teacher—a source of information. Our schools have survived as schools in spite of the efforts of other institutions—social reformers, clerics, politicians, labor unions —to use school children as a captive constituency for indoctrination. These schools have succeeded, albeit unevenly, to turn out informed and inquiring citizens, and these citizens have advanced an American way of life that has become a wonder to other nations of the world. School can contribute to a broader understanding of this way of life, but in the final analysis, it is the American way of life that shapes the uses of the information gained by pupils in school.

APPENDIX

Method Used to Compile the List of
Curriculum Classics—by Angela E. Fraley

In working through original sources for an historical dissertation, I found that a succession of people had been saying the same things for at least a hundred years. Knowledge of this literature can put all of the issues in perspective.

A list of twenty-three curriculum classics seemed to sort itself out. A classic was defined as a work that had a specific impact on the thinking of its time, or functioned as a turning point document in curriculum theory development, or endured as a widely used referent piece. It seemed reasonable to include only works that are at least ten years old. The list was circulated to all who attended the meeting of Professors of Curriculum at the ASCD Annual Meeting in Miami on March 12–13, 1976. With seven additions and two deletions, the list is appended.

A tally of the thirty-nine edited copies returned in Miami brought suggestions for fifty-four additions and seventeen deletions. Most of the additions were singly suggested, only nine of them being added by more than two people. Additional works by Dewey were recommended. A choice had to be made. Four veteran professors added Morrison's *Practice of Teaching in Secondary School* as "one of the classics of this century"—a monumental work that had never come to my attention. Taba's *Curriculum Development, Theory and Practice* was added on fifteen of the edited lists. Rugg, L. T. Hopkins, Alberty, and various reports and yearbooks received multiple mention, all worthy of special investigation; but limiting the list to a workable introductory number forced selection of one or two most used in each era.

Most of the items that were singly deleted had heavy counteracting approval, and they remain on the list. Critiques that do not carry accompanying formulative curriculum recommendations were excluded as "more suitably reserved for course work." Other items were suggested for exclusion not because they were deemed unworthy, but for duplication of content or for substitution of another work by the same author. There were also some suggested exclusions indicating that the individual felt the impact of the particular work had been negative, e.g., those recommending return to the disciplines. The purpose of this list was not to choose for negative or positive impact, but for strength of impact—the fact that the work influenced a powerful group or an era of curriculum thought.

The list is presented for consideration as a requirement for thorough study by all students of curriculum, regardless of their specialization, before they proceed too far into their graduate course work. It is intended not as a total program requirement, but as a starter to serve as *background* for study of current writings properly stressed in course work, or collateral writings properly stressed in specialized course work. It is also not intended to substitute for courses in the history of education where Cubberley's *Public Education in the United States* (1919) and Cremin's *Transformation of the School* (1961) are logically included.

The list is short and focuses on widely recognized works in the curriculum field covering the major issues since 1900. An entering student can easily work through it quickly during his first semester knowing that the time and effort will be well spent and that the knowledge will serve him well. There is leeway for users to add, delete, and/or substitute as their individuality dictates. The important thing is that some direction is provided to initiates in the field of graduate study in curriculum.

Curriculum Classics—1894–1964—A Selected List.
By Angela E. Fraley

1894 Parker, Francis W. *Talks on Pedagogics*. New York: E. L.
      Kellogg & Co., 1894. (491p) (reprinted—New York:
      Arno Press, 1969).
1897 Dewey, John. "My Pedagogic Creed." *The School Journal*,
      Vol. LIV, No. 3, (January 16, 1897), 77–80. (included in
      Dworkin, Martin S. *Dewey on Education*. New York:
      Teachers College, Columbia University, 1959.) (134p)
1902 Dewey, John. *The Child and the Curriculum*. Chicago:
      The University of Chicago Press, 1902. (20p) (included
      in Dworkin, Martin S. *Dewey on Education*. New York:
      Teachers College, Columbia University, 1959). (134p)
1905 Bagley, William C. *The Educative Process*. New York:
      The Macmillan Company, 1905. (358p)
1910 Dewey, John. *How We Think*. New York: D. C. Heath &
      Co., 1910. (224p)
1916 Dewey, John. *Democracy and Education*. New York: The
      Macmillan Co., 1916. (reprinted—New York: The Free
      Press, 1966. [378p])
1918 Bobbitt, (John) Franklin. *The Curriculum*. New York:
      Houghton Mifflin Company, 1918. (295p) (reprinted—
      New York: Arno Press, 1972).
1918 Commission on the Reorganization of Secondary Educa-
      tion of the National Education Association. *Cardinal
      Principles of Secondary Education*. Washington, D.C.:
      Department of the Interior, Bureau of Education, Bul-
      letin, 1918, No. 35. (32p)
1918 Kilpatrick, William Heard. *The Project Method*. New
      York: Teachers College, Columbia University, 1918.
      (18p) (reprinted from Teachers College Record, Vol.
      XIX, No. 4, September 1918).
1923 Charters, W. W. *Curriculum Construction*. New York:
      The Macmillan Company, 1923. (352p) (reprinted—
      New York: Arno Press, 1972).
1926 Morrison, Henry C. *The Practice of Teaching in the Sec-
      ondary School*. Chicago: The University of Chicago
      Press, 1926. (661p)

1926   Kilpatrick, William Heard. *Foundations of Method*. New York: The Macmillan Company, 1926. (383p) (reprinted —New York: Arno Press, 1972).

1926   National Society for the Study of Education. Twenty-Sixth Yearbook. Part I, *Curriculum Making: Past and Present*. Part II, *The Foundations of Curriculum Making*. Bloomington, Illinois: Public School Publishing Co., 1926. (475p, 212p) (reprinted—New York: Arno Press, 1970 [ref: Harold Rugg])

1932   Counts, George S. *Dare the School Build a New Social Order?* New York: John Day Company, 1932. (56p) (reprinted—New York: Arno Press, 1969).

1935   Caswell, Hollis L. and Campbell, Doak S. *Curriculum Development*. New York: American Book Company, 1935. (600p)

1938   Dewey, John. *Experience and Education*. New York: Collier Books, 1963 [1938]. (91p)

1942   Aikin, Wilford M. *The Story of the Eight-Year Study*. New York: Harper & Brothers, 1942. (157p)

1944   National Education Association. Educational Policies Commission. *Education for All American Youth*. Washington, D.C.: National Education Association and the Association of School Administrators, 1944. (421p) (also rev. ed. 1952)

1945   Harvard Committee on the Objectives of a General Education in a Free Society. *General Education in a Free Society*. Cambridge: Harvard University Press, 1945. (267p)

1946   Miel, Alice. *Changing the Curriculum: A Social Process*. New York: D. Appleton-Century Company, Inc., 1946. (242p)

1946   Caswell, Hollis L., ed. *The American High School: Its Responsibility and Opportunity*. (Eighth Yearbook of the John Dewey Society) New York: Harper & Brothers Publishers, 1946. (264p)

1947   Stratemeyer, Florence B.; Forkner, Hamden L.; and McKim, Margaret G. *Developing a Curriculum for Modern Living*. New York: Teachers College, Columbia University, 1947. (558p)

1949 Tyler, Ralph W. *Basic Principles of Curriculum and In-struction.* Chicago: The University of Chicago Press, 1949. (128p)

1950 Smith, B. O.; Stanley, Wm. O.; and Shores, J. Harlan. *Fundamentals of Curriculum Development.* Yonkers-on-Hudson: World Book Company, 1950. (780p)

1956 Bloom, Benjamin S., ed. *Taxonomy of Educational Objec-tives. Handbook I: Cognitive Domain.* New York: David McKay Company, Inc., 1956. (207p)

1959 Conant, James B. *The American High School Today.* New York: McGraw-Hill Book Company, Inc., 1959. (141p)

1960 Bruner, Jerome S. *The Process of Education.* Cambridge: Harvard University Press, 1960. (97p)

1962 Taba, Hilda. *Curriculum Development: Theory and Prac-tice.* New York: Harcourt, Brace & World, 1962. (526p)

1964 Broudy, Harry S.; Smith, B. O.; and Burnett, Joe R. *De-mocracy and Excellence in American Secondary Educa-tion.* Chicago: Rand McNally & Company, 1964. (302p)

BIBLIOGRAPHY

Aikin, Wilford M. "The Eight-Year Study: If We Were to Do It Again." *Progressive Education*, XXXI (October 1953), pp. 11–14.

Aikin, Wilford M. *The Story of the Eight-Year Study*. New York: Harper & Brothers, 1942. (see entry under Progressive Education Association)

Alberty, Harold B. "An Appraisal of Dewey's Aphorism, 'Education is Life' "—Abstract, National Education Association, *Department of Superintendence, Official Report*, 1930, p. 152.

Alberty, Harold B. "The Core Program in the High School." A Recording. Educational Recording Services, 6430 Sherbourne Drive, Los Angeles, Calif., 90056. Lecture recorded in December of 1951.

Alberty, Harold B. "Designing Programs to Meet the Common Needs of Youth." *Adapting the Secondary School Program to the Needs of Youth*. Fifty-second Yearbook of the National Society for the Study of Education, Part I. Chicago: University of Chicago Press, 1953, pp. 118–140.

Alberty, Harold B. "My Friend, 'Hank' Hullfish." *Educational Theory*, XIII (July 1963), pp. 189–191.

Alberty, Harold B., chairman, Committee on Preparation of Core Teachers. *Preparation of Core Teachers for Secondary Schools*. Washington, D.C.: Association for Supervision and Curriculum Development, 1955.

Alberty, Harold B. "The Progressive Education Movement." *Educational Research Bulletin*, VIII (April 17, 1929), pp. 163–169.

Alberty, Harold B. "Supervision as a Means of Integrating the Total Secondary School Program." *Schoolmen's Week Proceedings*, University of Pennsylvania, XX (April 1933), pp. 269–274.

Alberty, Harold B., and Thayer, V. T. *Supervision in the Secondary School*. New York: D. C. Heath & Co., 1931.

Ambrosino, Lillian. "The Hamilton School Experience." In *Blowing on a Candle: The Flavor of Change*. Edited by David Whiting. Newton, Massachusetts: Newton Public Schools, [1972].

Bourne, Randolph S. *The Gary Schools*. New York: Houghton Mifflin Company, 1916.

Broder, Dorothy Elizabeth. "Life Adjustment Education: An Historical Study of a Program of the United States Office of Education, 1945–1954." Unpublished Ed.D. dissertation, Teachers College, Columbia University, 1976.

Bruner, Jerome S. *The Process of Education*. Cambridge: Harvard University Press, 1960.

Bullough, Robert V., Jr. "Harold B. Alberty and Boyd H. Bode: Pioneers in Curriculum Theory." Unpublished Ph.D. dissertation, The Ohio State University, 1976.

Campbell, Jack K. *Colonel Francis W. Parker: The Children's Crusader*. New York: Teachers College Press, Columbia University, 1967.

Caswell, Hollis L.; and Campbell, Doak S. *Curriculum Development*. New York: American Book Company, 1935.

Charters, W. W., Jr.; and Jones, John E. "On the Risk of Appraising Non-Events in Program Evaluation." *Educational Researcher*, II, No. 11 (November 1973), pp. 5–7.

Coleman, James S. et al. *Equality of Educational Opportunity*. Washington, D.C.: Department of Health, Education, and Welfare, Office of Education, 1966.

Commission on the Reorganization of Secondary Education of the National Education Association. *Cardinal Principles of Secondary Education*. Department of the Interior, Bureau of Education, Bulletin, 1918, No. 35. Washington, D.C.: U.S. Government Printing Office, 1918.

Counts, George S. *Dare the School Build a New Social Order?* New York: John Day Co., 1932.

Cremin, Lawrence A. *The American Common School: An Historic Conception*. New York: Teachers College, Columbia University, 1951.

Cremin, Lawrence A. *American Education: The Colonial Experience 1607–1783*. New York: Harper & Row, 1970.

Cremin, Lawrence A. *The Transformation of the School: Progressivism in American Education 1876–1957*. New York: Alfred A. Knopf, 1961.

deLima, Agnes. *Democracy's High School*. New York: Teachers College, Columbia University, 1941.

Dewey, John. *The Child and the Curriculum*. Chicago: The University of Chicago Press, 1902. In Martin S. Dworkin, ed., *Dewey on Education*. New York: Teachers College, Columbia University, 1959.

Dewey, John. *Democracy and Education*. New York: The Free Press, 1966 [1916].

Dewey, John. "My Pedagogic Creed." in *The School Journal*, Vol. LIV, No. 3 (January 16, 1897), pp. 77–80.

Dewey, John. *Schools of To-Morrow*. New York: E. P. Dutton & Company, 1915.

Diederich, Paul B. "The Eight-Year Study: More Comments." *Progressive Education*, Vol. 28, No. 5 (March 1951), pp. 163–164.

Dworkin, Martin S. *Dewey on Education*. New York: Teachers College, Columbia University, 1959.

Educational Policies Commission. *Education for All American Youth*. Washington, D.C.: National Education Association, 1944.

Evans, Alison. "The Meadowbrook Experience." in *Blowing on a Candle: The Flavor of Change*. Edited by David Whiting. Newton, Massachusetts: Newton Public Schools, [1972].

Federal Security Agency. *Developing Life Adjustment Education in a Local School*. Office of Education Circular No. 253. Washington, D.C.: Federal Security Agency, 1949.

Federal Security Agency. *Vitalizing Secondary Education*. Office of Education Bulletin 1951, No. 3. Washington, D.C.: Federal Security Agency, 1951.

Flexner, Abraham; and Bachman, Frank P. *The Gary Schools: A General Account*. Part I. New York: General Education Board, 1918.

Flexner, Abraham. *I Remember*. New York: Simon and Schuster, 1940.

Ford Foundation. *Decade of Experiment: The Fund for the Ad-

vancement of Education 1951–1961. New York: Ford Foundation Fund for the Advancement of Education, 1961.

Ford Foundation. *A Foundation Goes to School: The Ford Foundation Comprehensive School Improvement Program 1960–1970.* New York: Ford Foundation, 1972.

Ford Foundation. *Report of the Study for the Ford Foundation on Policy and Program.* Detroit: Ford Foundation, 1949.

Fraley, Angela E. "Core Curriculum: An Epic in the History of Educational Reform." Unpublished Ed.D. dissertation, Teachers College, Columbia University, 1977.

Gary, Indiana. Rossman, John G. *The Auditorium and its Administration.* Gary, Indiana: Board of Education, 1927.

Gary, Indiana, Board of Education. *Information Concerning Work-Study-Play Schools.* Circular of Information to Applicants for Teaching Positions. Gary: Board of Education, 1925–1926.

Gary, Indiana, Board of Education. *The Taxpayer and the Gary Public Schools.* Gary: Board of Education, 1934.

Giles, H. H.; McCutchen, S. P.; and Zechiel, A. N. *Exploring the Curriculum.* New York: Harper & Brothers, 1942. (See entry under Progressive Education Association)

Goodlad, John I.; Klein, M. Frances; and associates. *Behind the Classroom Door.* Worthington, Ohio: Charles A. Jones Publishing Co., 1970.

Heffron, Ida Cass. *Francis Wayland Parker.* Los Angeles: Ivan Deach, Jr., Publishers, 1934.

Johnson, Mauritz, Jr. "The Rise and Fall of Life Adjustment." *Saturday Review,* XLIV (March 18, 1961), pp. 46–47.

Kozol, Jonathan. "A Junior High That's Like a College." *New York Times Magazine,* October 29, 1967, p. 32.

Mayhew, Katherine Camp; and Edwards, Anna Camp. *The Dewey School.* New York: D. Appleton-Century Company, Inc., 1936.

Mississippi. State Department of Education. *A Guide for Curriculum Planning.* Mississippi Program for the Improvement of Instruction, Bulletin No. 3, October 1936. Jackson: State Department of Education, 1936.

Mississippi. State Department of Education. *Procedures for Pro-*

duction of Curriculum Materials. Mississippi Program for the Improvement of Instruction, Bulletin No. 2, October 1935. Jackson: State Department of Education, 1935.

Mississippi. State Department of Education. *Study Program.* Mississippi Program for the Improvement of Instruction, Bulletin No. 1, October 1934. Jackson: State Department of Education, 1934.

Naumberg, Joan. Editorial in *Lincoln Lore.* A magazine of literature and art issued by the pupils of Lincoln School of Teachers College, New York City. Vol. XV, No. 3 (April 1933), pp. 12–13.

Neill, A. S. *Summerhill.* New York: Hart Publishing Co., 1960.

News Bulletin was the name on the publications that preceded the *Curriculum Journal* of the Stociety for Curriculum Study.

Newton Public Schools. *Blowing on a Candle: A Study of Educational Change in the Newton Public Schools 1959–1969.* Edited by David Whiting. Newton, Massachusetts: Newton Public Schools, [1972].

Newton Public Schools. *Blowing on a Candle: The Flavor of Change.* Edited by David Whiting. Newton, Massachusetts: Newton Public Schools, [1972].

Ohio State University School. "Grades Seven to Twelve—Ohio State University School." *Educational Research Bulletin,* XV, No. 2 February 12, 1936, pp. 29–66.

Ohio State University School. *A Handbook for University School Parents.* Columbus: College of Education, The Ohio State University, 1954.

Ohio State University School, Class of 1938. *Were We Guinea Pigs?* New York: H. Holt & Co., 1938.

Oppleman, Dan. "Development of the Revised Curriculum Program in Virginia Secondary Schools." Unpublished Ed.D. dissertation, George Peabody College for Teachers, 1955.

Overton, Harvey. "The Rise and Fall of the Core Curriculum." in *Schools for the Middle Years: Readings.* Edited by George C. Stoumbis and Alvin W. Howard. Scranton, Pennsylvania: International Textbook Co., 1969.

Parker, Francis W. *Talks on Pedagogics.* New York: E. L. Kellogg & Co., 1894. (reprinted: New York: Arno Press, 1969)

Parker, Francis W. *Talks on Teaching*. Reported by Lelia E. Partridge. New York: A. S. Barnes & Co., [cop. 1883].

Progressive Education Association. Commission on the Relation of School and College. *Adventure in American Education*. Vol. I, *The Story of the Eight-Year Study*, by Wilford M. Aikin; Vol. II, *Exploring the Curriculum*, by H. H. Giles, S. P. Mc-Cutchen, and A. N. Zechiel; Vol. III, *Appraising and Recording Student Progress*, by Eugene R. Smith, Ralph W. Tyler, et. al.; Vol. IV, *Did They Succeed in College?* by Dean Chamberlin, Enid Chamberlin, Neal E. Drought, and William E. Scott; Vol. V, *Thirty Schools Tell Their Story*. New York: Harper & Brothers, 1942.

Progressive Education Association. *Science in General Education*. New York: D. Appleton-Century Company, Inc., 1938.

Public Administration Service. *The Public School System of Gary, Indiana*. Chicago: Publications Division of the Public Administration Service, 1955.

Ravitch, Diane. *The Great School Wars*. New York: Basic Books, Inc., 1974.

Redefer, Frederick L. "The Eight Year Study—Eight Years Later." Unpublished Ed.D. dissertation, Teachers College, Columbia University, 1952.

Rice, Joseph Mayer. *The Public-School System of the United States*. New York: The Century Company, 1893. (reprinted: New York: Arno Press, 1969)

Rush, Benjamin. "Of the Mode of Education Proper in a Republic" (1798). in *Beaver Island Reprints in the History of Education*, HE#220. Bergenfield, N.J.: Beaver Island Publishing Co., Inc., 1967.

Seguel, Mary Louise. *The Curriculum Field: Its Formative Years*. New York: Teachers College Press, 1966.

Silberman, Charles E. *Crisis in the Classroom*. New York: Random House, 1970.

Spears, Harold B. *The Emerging High School Curriculum and Its Direction*. New York: American Book Company, 1940.

Tyack, David B. *Turning Points in American Educational History*. Waltham, Massachusetts: Blaisdell Publishing Company, 1967.

Vars, Gordon F. "Can Team Teaching Save the Core Curriculum?" *Phi Delta Kappan*, XLVII (January 1966), pp. 258–262.

Virginia. State Board of Education. "Materials of Instruction Suggested for the First Year of the Core Curriculum of Virginia Secondary Schools," Richmond, September 1938. (mimeographed)

Virginia. State Board of Education. "Materials of Instruction Suggested for the Fourth Year of the Core Curriculum of Virginia Secondary Schools," Richmond, [1941]. (mimeographed)

Virginia. State Board of Education. "Materials of Instruction Suggested for the Second Year of the Core Curriculum of Virginia Secondary Schools," Richmond, 1938. (mimeographed)

Virginia. State Board of Education. "Materials of Instruction Suggested for the Third Year of the Core Curriculum of Virginia Secondary Schools," Richmond, 1939. (mimeographed)

Virginia. State Board of Education. *Tentative Course of Study for the Core Curriculum of Virginia Secondary Schools Grade VIII.* Bulletin XVII, No. 2 (August 1934). Richmond: Virginia State Division of Purchase and Printing, 1934.

Virginia. State Board of Education. "(Additional) Tentative Materials of Instruction Suggested for the Core Curriculum of Virginia Secondary Schools. Grade VIII." Richmond, October 1936. (mimeographed)

Virginia. State Board of Education. "Tentative Materials of Instruction Suggested for the Core Curriculum of Virginia Secondary Schools, Grade IX." Richmond, September 1936. (mimeographed)

Whiting, David. "Final Report on the Supplementary Grant, January 1966–August 1968." Newton, Massachusetts: Newton Public Schools, January 1970. (mimeographed)

Willis, Margaret. *The Guinea Pigs after Twenty Years. A Follow-Up Study of the Class of 1938 of the University School, Ohio State University.* Columbus: State University Press, 1961.

Wright, Grace S. *Block-Time Classes and the Core Program in the Junior High School.* Office of Education Bulletin 1958, No. 6. Washington, D.C.: Department of Health, Education, and Welfare, 1958.

Wright, Grace S. *Core Curriculum Development: Problems and*

Practices. Office of Education Bulletin 1952, No. 5. Washington, D.C.: Federal Security Agency, 1952.

Wright, Grace S. *Core Curriculum in Public High Schools: An Inquiry into Practices, 1949*. Office of Education Bulletin 1950, No. 5. Washington, D.C.: Federal Security Agency, 1950.

Wright, Grace S., and Greer, Edith S. *The Junior High School: A Survey of Grades 7–8–9 in Junior High Schools and Junior-Senior High Schools, 1959–60*. Office of Education Bulletin 1963, No. 32. Washington, D.C.: U.S. Government Printing Office, 1963.

Zapf, Rosalind M. *Democratic Process in the Secondary Classroom*. Englewood Cliffs, N.J.: Prentice-Hall, Inc., 1959.

INDEX